OTHER BOOKS BY OGDEN NASH

⌘ ⌘ ⌘

HARD LINES

⌘

FREE WHEELING

⌘

HAPPY DAYS

⌘

THE PRIMROSE PATH

⌘

THE BAD PARENTS' GARDEN OF VERSE

⌘

I'M A STRANGER HERE MYSELF

THE FACE
IS FAMILIAR

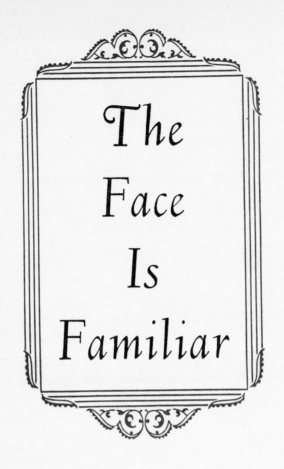

The Face Is Familiar

THE SELECTED VERSE OF

OGDEN NASH

BOSTON

Little, Brown and Company · 1940

Published November 1940
Reprinted November 1940

PRINTED IN THE UNITED STATES OF AMERICA

FOR FRANCES

And now to settle for the years,
That flew like frightened birds;
As fee for ten of happiness
I offer ten of words.

To the editors and proprietors of the following publications, in which many of these verses first appeared, the author is most grateful: the *American Magazine*, the *New York American*, *Child Life*, the *Continental Distilling Corporation Recipe Book*, "The Conning Tower," *Cosmopolitan*, *Delineator*, *Harper's Bazaar*, *Life*, the *New Outlook*, the *New Yorker*, *Red Book*, the *Saturday Evening Post*, and the *Saturday Review of Literature*.

CONTENTS

· xi ·

· xiii ·

· xiv ·

· xvii ·

· xix ·

· xxi ·

THE FACE
IS FAMILIAR

TWO AND ONE ARE A PROBLEM

Dear Miss Dix, I am a young man of half-past thirty-
seven.
My friends say I am not unattractive, though to be
kind and true is what I have always striven.
I have brown hair, green eyes, a sensitive mouth and a
winning natural exuberance,
And, at the waist, a barely noticeable protuberance.
I am open-minded about beverages so long as they are
grape, brandy or malt,
And I am generous to practically any fault.
Well Miss Dix not to beat around the bush, there is a
certain someone who thinks I am pretty nice,
And I turn to you for advice.
You see, it started when I was away on the road
And returned to find a pair of lovebirds had taken up
their abode in my abode.
Well I am not crazy about lovebirds, but I must say
they looked very sweet in their gilded cage,
And their friendship had reached an advanced stage,
And I had just forgiven her who of the feathered
fiancés was the donor of
When the houseboy caught a lost lovebird in the yard
that we couldn't locate the owner of.
So then we had three, and it was no time for flippancy,
Because everybody knows that a lovebird without its
own lovebird to love will pine away and die of the
discrepancy,
So we bought a fourth lovebird for the third lovebird
and they sat around very cozily beak to beak
And then the third lovebird that we had provided the

fourth lovebird for to keep it from dying died at
the end of the week,
So we were left with an odd lovebird and it was no time
for flippancy,
Because a lovebird without its own lovebird to love will
pine away and die of the discrepancy,
So we had to buy a fifth lovebird to console the fourth
lovebird that we had bought to keep the third
lovebird contented,
And now the fourth lovebird has lost its appetite, and,
Miss Dix, I am going demented.
I don't want to break any hearts, but I got to know
where I'm at;
Must I keep on buying lovebirds, Miss Dix, or do you
think it would be all right to buy a cat?

TABOO TO BOOT

One bliss for which
There is no match
Is when you itch
To up and scratch.

Yet doctors and dowagers deprecate scratching,
Society ranks it with spitting and snatching,
And medical circles consistently hold
That scratching's as wicked as feeding a cold.

Hell's flame burns unquenched 'neath how many a
stocking
On account of to scratch in a salon is shocking!

Avid ankles deprived of the fingernail's kiss
For fear of a dermatological hiss!

> 'Neath tile or thatch
> That man is rich
> Who has a scratch
> For every itch.

Ho, squirmers and writhers, how long will ye suffer
The medical tyrant, the social rebuffer!
On the edge of the door let our shoulderblades rub,
Let the drawing room now be as free as the tub!
Let us scratch in the presence of multitudes medical
And if they object, let us call them unedical!
So the ogres of ivy and ringworm and allergies
We'll scratch to the stature of abject apologies!

> I'm greatly attached
> To Barbara Frietchie.
> I bet she scratched
> When she was itchy.

THE SEA-GULL

Hark to the whimper of the sea-gull;
He weeps because he's not an ea-gull.
Suppose you were, you silly sea-gull,
Could you explain it to your she-gull?

Consider the man without a watch.
He is like a soda without Scotch.
Of the male character I can quickly give you the gist;
It is the reach for the pocket or the glance at the wrist.
From the moment they are fledglings
Males discipline themselves with timings and schedul-
    ings.
Be they lovers, golfers, or railroad engineers,
Time is the essential ingredient in their careers,
And there is nothing more surly
Than a watchless man who doesn't know whether he is
    late or early,
And clocks are no good to him because he can't take
    them along,
And anyhow a clock is only something that you com-
    pare with your watch and find the clock is several
    minutes wrong.
If there is one thing that every man thinks how sub-
    lime it is,
It is to know what time it is.
Women don't like watches.
They feel about them as they do about facial blemishes
    or blotches.
They only tolerate them when they are embedded in
    brooches or bracelets or belts,
Or in some way disguised to look like something else.
Yes, it's obvious that women don't like them or need
    them,
Because with women's watches you need a microscope
    and a map to read them.

Time is something they resent, and they fight it with
    peculiarly feminine resistance;
They refuse to acknowledge its existence.
In this sexual conflict in attitude toward time who am
    I to tip the scales?
I only know that more males wait for females than fe-
    males wait for males.

MR. ARTESIAN'S CONSCIENTIOUSNESS

Once there was a man named Mr. Artesian and his ac-
    tivity was tremendous,
And he grudged every minute away from his desk be-
    cause the importance of his work was so stupen-
    dous;
And he had one object all sublime,
Which was to save simply oodles of time.
He figured that sleeping eight hours a night meant that
    if he lived to be seventy-five he would have spent
    twenty-five years not at his desk but in bed,
So he cut his slumber to six hours which meant he only
    lost eighteen years and nine months instead,
And he figured that taking ten minutes for breakfast
    and twenty minutes for luncheon and half an hour
    for dinner meant that he spent three years, two
    months and fifteen days at the table,
So that by subsisting solely on bouillon cubes which he
    swallowed at his desk to save this entire period he
    was able,
And he figured that at ten minutes a day he spent a
    little over six months and ten days shaving,

So he grew a beard, which gave him a considerable saving,
And you might think that now he might have been
satisfied, but no, he wore a thoughtful frown,
Because he figured that at two minutes a day he would
spend thirty-eight days and a few minutes in elevators just traveling up and down,
So as a final timesaving device he stepped out the window of his office, which happened to be on the
fiftieth floor,
And one of his partners asked "Has he vertigo?" and
the other glanced out and down and said "Oh no,
only about ten feet more."

I YIELD TO MY LEARNED BROTHER,
or
IS THERE A CANDLESTICK MAKER
IN THE HOUSE?

The doctor gets you when you're born,
The preacher, when you marry,
And the lawyer lurks with costly clerks
If too much on you carry.
Professional men, they have no cares;
Whatever happens, they get theirs.

You can't say When
To professional men,
For it's always When to they;
They go out and golf
With the big bad wolf

In the most familiar way.
Hard times for them contain no terrors;
Their income springs from human errors.

The butcher you can do without,
And eke the jolly baker,
And it's childish sport if you wish to thwart
The plaintive candlestick maker,
For they are not professional men,
And we can spare them now and then.

But the noblest lord is ushered in
By a practising physician,
And the humblest lout is ushered out
By a certified mortician.
And in between, they find their foyers
Alive with summonses from lawyers.

Oh, would my parents long ago
Had memorized this motto!
For then might I, their offspring, buy
A Rolls or an Isotto.
But now I fear I never can,
For I am no professional man.

You can't say When
To professional men,
For it's always When to they;
They were doing fine
In '29,
And they're doing fine today.
One beacon doth their paths illumine,
To wit: To err is always humine.

REFLECTION ON THE PASSAGE OF TIME, ITS INEVITABILITY AND ITS QUIRKS

In nineteen hunderd
Jeunes filles wondered.

THE DROP OF A HAT

Darling, what is that?
That, angel, is a hat.
Are you positive? Are you certain?
Are you sure it's not a curtain?
Shall you really place your head in it?
How's for keeping cake or bread in it?
Do not wear it on your head;
Find some other use instead.
Say a cloth for drying dishes,
Or a net for catching fishes,
Or a veil by night to veto
The bill of the mosquito?
Darling, what is that?
Are you sure it is a hat?
And if so, what was the matter
With the hatter?
Was he troubled? Was he ill?
Was he laughing fit to kill?
Oh, what was on his mind
As he designed?
Had he gone without his supper?
Was he dressing in an upper?
Did he plot a wily plan

To annoy his fellow man?
Is its aspect, rear and frontal,
Intended to disgruntle,
Or was it accidental
And is he now repental?
Are memoirs of the brim
Now agony to him?
Do visions of the crown
Drag his spirits down?
Oh, may the Furies batter
That eleven-fingered hatter!
May doom and gloom enswaddle
The creator of this model!
I hope he made a lot of them,
That dozens he has got of them;
I hope he has a harem,
And all his spouses warem.

THE CENTIPEDE

I objurgate the centipede,
A bug we do not really need.
At sleepy-time he beats a path
Straight to the bedroom or the bath.
You always wallop where he's not,
Or, if he is, he makes a spot.

WHAT'S THE MATTER, HAVEN'T YOU GOT ANY SENSE OF HUMOR?

There is at least one thing I would less rather have in
    the neighborhood than a gangster,
And that one thing is a practical prankster.
I feel that we should differ more sharply than Monta-
    gues and Capulets or York and Lancaster,
Me and a practical prancaster.
If there is a concentration camp in limbo, that is the
    spot for which I nominate them,
Not because I don't like them, but simply because I
    abominate them.
The born practical prankster starts out in early youth
    by offering people a chair,
And when they sit down it isn't there,
And he is delighted and proceeds to more complicated
    wheezes,
Such as ten cent X-rays to see through people's clothes
    with and powders to give them itches and sneezes,
And his boutonnière is something that people get
    squirted in the eye out of,
And their beds are what he makes apple pie out of.
Then as he matures he widens his scope,
And he is no longer content to present people with ex-
    ploding cigars and chocolate creams with centers
    of soap,
So he dresses up as an Oriental potentate and reviews
    the British fleet,
Or collects a little group of kinsprits and a few pick-
    axes and a STREET CLOSED sign and digs up a busy
    street,

And if people are jumpy about their past or present
   private lives he hints that he is writing his memoirs
   and is devoting an entire chapter to their particular skeleton,
And finally he reaches the apex of his career when he
   slips into somebody's bathroom and fills up all the
   modern conveniences with water and then adds
   raspberry gelatin.
I have recently read with complete satisfaction of a
   practical prankster two of whose friends had just
   been married,
Which was of course in itself simply a challenge to be
   harried,
And it was a challenge he was eager to meet,
And he went to the roof of their hotel and tied a rope
   around his waist and a colleague lowered him to
   where he could clash a pair of cymbals outside the
   window of the nuptial suite,
And he weighed two hundred and eighty pounds and
   the rope broke,
And that to my mind is the perfect practical joke.

LINES TO BE MUMBLED AT OVINGTON'S

Mr. and Mrs. F. X. Pleasants
Request the honor of my presence,
On Saturday the twenty-fourth
To watch their daughter, Barbara North,
Succumb in holy matrimony
To Mr. Maximilian Coney.

· 13 ·

A murrain on you, Mr. and Mrs. Pleasants!
I hope you turn into friends of Annie Besant's!

Bishop Apse will do the trick;
He's just the kind that mothers pick.
He has a noble velvet voice
That makes a mother's heart rejoice
And fills a mother's handkerchief
With briny evidence of grief.
A murrain on you too, old Bishop Apse!
I hope you get caught in some vicious moral lapse!

The ushers in their coats of black
Will lead old ladies forth and back,
While bridesmaids in their flowery frocks
Bloom round the bride like hollyhocks.
Who knows but what some sidelong glance
Will propagate a new romance?
A murrain on every bridesmaid and every usher!
I hope they all get spattered with oil from a gusher!

I'll wish some wishes for Mr. Coney
In honor of his matrimony.
I wish him moths, I wish him mice,
I wish him cocktails lacking ice.
I wish him a life abrupt and lonely,
I wish him a wife in title only.
A murrain, a murrain upon you, Maximilian!
If I wish you one death before evening I wish you a bil-
    lion!

What have I left for Barbara North

Who changes her name on the twenty-fourth?
A hundred theater-ticket stubs,
Receipted bills from supper clubs,
A dozen notes whose theme is If,
Some lipstick on a handkerchief—
A lesser soul of spite would be a harborer;
Not I. No murrain at all upon you, Barbara!

INVOCATION

("Smoot Plans Tariff Ban on
Improper Books" — *News Item*)

Senator Smoot (Republican, Ut.)
Is planning a ban on smut.
Oh rooti-ti-toot for Smoot of Ut.
And his reverent occiput.
Smite, Smoot, smite for Ut.,
Grit your molars and do your dut.,
Gird up your l—ns,
Smite h–p and th–gh,
We'll all be Kansas
By and by.

Smite, Smoot, for the Watch and Ward,
For Hiram Johnson and Henry Ford,
For Bishop Cannon and John D., Junior,
For Governor Pinchot of Pennsylvunia,
For John S. Sumner and Elder Hays
And possibly Edward L. Bernays,

For Orville Poland and Ella Boole,
For Mother Machree and the Shelton pool.
When smut's to be smitten
Smoot will smite
For G–d, for country,
And Fahrenheit.

Senator Smoot is an institute
Not to be bribed with pelf;
He guards our homes from erotic tomes
By reading them all himself.
Smite, Smoot, smite for Ut.,
They're smuggling smut from Balt. to Butte!
Strongest and sternest
Of your s–x
Scatter the scoundrels
From Can. to Mex.!

Smite, Smoot, for Smedley Butler,
For any good man by the name of Cutler,
Smite for the W.C.T.U.,
For Rockne's team and for Leader's crew,
For Florence Coolidge and Admiral Byrd,
For Billy Sunday and John D., Third,
For Grantland Rice and for Albie Booth,
For the Woman's Auxiliary of Duluth,
Smite, Smoot,
Be rugged and rough,
Smut if smitten
Is front-page stuff.

I find it very difficult to enthuse
Over the current news.
The daily paper is so harrowing that it is costly even at
the modest price of two cents;
It lands on your doorstep with a thud and you can't
bear to look at it but neither can you forbear, because it lies there with all the gruesome fascina-
tion of something that fell or jumped from the
thirtieth floor and lit on a picket fence.
And you think that perhaps a leisurely perusal of some
unsensational literary magazine will ease the stress,
And there you find an article presenting a foolproof
plan for the defense of some small nation which
unfortunately happened to get swallowed up by a
nation not so small just as the article presenting
the foolproof plan for its defense slid off the press.
And you furtively eye your radio which crouches in the
corner like a hyena ready to spring,
And you know that what you want is Baby Snooks or
Dr. I.Q. and you know that what you will get is
Elmer Davis or a European roundup or Raymond
Gram Swing.
Wherever you turn, whatever escapist stratagem you
use,
All you get is news,
And just when you think that at least the outlook is
so black that it can grow no blacker, it worsens,
And that is why I do not like to get the news, because
there has never been an era when so many things
were going so right for so many of the wrong per-
sons.

Pendleton Birdsong was a wise child.

⁓

He knew a hawk from a handsaw and a vaccination from a vacation.

⁓

He knew which side his bread was buttered on and enough to come in out of a monsoon.

⁓

At the age of three he had mastered the principles of higher mathematics.

⁓

When attacked by measles he spent several improving hours in counting his spots and multiplying them by the cube root of seven, thirteen, and one hundred and twenty-nine and one half.

⁓

He could tell anyone who would listen just why parallel lines never meet.

⁓

Or, if they do, why they do.

⁓

He knew the difference between an egoist and an egotist and a gourmand and a gourmet and how to make out an income tax return.

⁓

Pendleton Birdsong was a wise child.

⁓

He knew his own father.

⁓

He was all fixed.

⁓

He said he was the wise child that knew its own father, and he was all fixed.

⁂

Senator Borah said Oh he was, was he, and how about The child is father of the man?

⁂

You should have seen Pendleton Birdsong's face.

⁂

He said he was going home to figure it out.

⁂

He said You knew how it was about repartee, you never could think of anything to say until you got home.

⁂

Then it came over you in a flash.

⁂

Senator Borah just leered and went off to embarrass the Administration.

⁂

Pendleton Birdsong sat down to uncomplicate this complication.

⁂

He said I am the wise child that knows its own father.

⁂

Now it seems that I am also father of the man.

⁂

That means Me after I have passed through adolescence and entered maturity.

⁂

Therefore I am my own father.

⁂

But I know my own father, and he's not me.

⁂

Maybe I had better ask him to make sure.

ᴄⱳ

He did, and he said he wasn't.

ᴄⱳ

He added that brothers and sisters had he none, but
Pendleton Birdsong's father was his father's son.

ᴄⱳ

That didn't get anybody anywhere much.

ᴄⱳ

Then Pendleton Birdsong remembered that he was not
yet a man, so he could not yet be his own father.

ᴄⱳ

Furthermore when he got to be a man he wouldn't be
a child, and it was a child that the man was to be
the son of.

ᴄⱳ

Even furthermore when he got to be a man he wouldn't
be a wise child, so he wouldn't know his father any
more.

ᴄⱳ

The child that he was now but wouldn't be when he
was a man would be his father.

ᴄⱳ

The father he wouldn't know any more would be himself.

ᴄⱳ

So he wouldn't know himself any more.

ᴄⱳ

By this time he didn't want to.

ᴄⱳ

He caught measles again and read Peter Rabbit instead
of counting his spots.

ᴄⱳ

He attracted much unfavorable attention in the neighborhood by trying to saw wood with a hawk.

ᛩ

He grew up to be a piano mover and had seventeen
children.

ᛩ

One day they all came to him and said they knew their
father.

ᛩ

He said he did too.

ᛩ

Mrs. Birdsong almost died.

SONG OF THE OPEN ROAD

I think that I shall never see
A billboard lovely as a tree.
Indeed, unless the billboards fall
I'll never see a tree at all.

LINES TO A WORLD-FAMOUS POET WHO
FAILED TO COMPLETE A WORLD-
FAMOUS POEM
or
COME CLEAN, MR. GUEST!

Oft when I'm sitting without anything to read waiting
for a train in a depot,
I torment myself with the poet's dictum that to make
a house a home, livin' is what it takes a heap o'.

Now, I myself should very much enjoy makin' my
　　house a home, but my brain keeps on a-goin'
　　clickety-click, clickety-click, clickety-click,
If Peter Piper picked a peck o' heap o' livin', what kind
　　of a peck o' heap o' livin' would Peter Piper pick?
Certainly a person doesn't need the brains of a Lin-
　　coln
To know that there are many kinds o' livin', just as
　　there are many kinds o' dancin' or huntin' or
　　fishin' or eatin' or drinkin'.
A philosophical poet should be specific
As well as prolific,
And I trust I am not being offensive
If I suggest that he should also be comprehensive.
You may if you like verify my next statement by send-
　　ing a stamped, self-addressed envelope to either
　　Dean Inge or Dean Gauss,
But meanwhile I ask you to believe that it takes a heap
　　of other things besides a heap o' livin' to make a
　　home out of a house.
To begin with, it takes a heap o' payin',
And you don't pay just the oncet, but agayin and
　　agayin and agayin.
Buyin' a stock is called speculatin' and buyin' a house
　　is called investin',
But the value of the stock or of the house fluctuates up
　　and down, generally down, just as an irresponsible
　　Destiny may destine.
Something else that your house takes a heap o', whether
　　the builder came from Sicily or Erin,
Is repairin',

In addition to which, gentle reader, I am sorry to say
you are little more than an imbecile or a cretin
If you think it doesn't take a heap o' heatin',
And unless you're spiritually allied to the little Dutch
boy who went around inspectin' dikes lookin' for
leaks to put his thumb in,
It takes a heap o' plumbin',
And if it's a house that you're hopin' to spend not just
today but tomorrow in,
It takes a heap o' borrowin'.
In a word, Macushla,
There's a scad o' things that to make a house a home it
takes not only a heap, or a peck, but at least a
bushela.

WHEN YOU SAY THAT, SMILE!
or
ALL RIGHT THEN, DON'T SMILE

When the odds are long,
And the game goes wrong,
Does your joie de vivre diminish?
Have you little delight
In an uphill fight?
Do you wince at a Garrison finish?
Then here's my hand, my trusty partner!
I've always wanted a good disheartener.

Oh, things are frequently what they seem,
And this is wisdom's crown:

Only the game fish swims upstream,
But the sensible fish swims down.

Well, how is your pulse
When a cad insults
The lady you're cavaliering?
Are you willing to wait
To retaliate
Till the cad is out of hearing?
Then here's my hand, my trusty companion,
And may neither one of us fall in a canyon.

For things are frequently what they seem,
And this is wisdom's crown:
Only the game fish swims upstream,
But the sensible fish swims down.

CHILDREN'S PARTY

May I join you in the doghouse, Rover?
I wish to retire till the party's over.
Since three o'clock I've done my best
To entertain each tiny guest;
My conscience now I've left behind me,
And if they want me, let them find me.
I blew their bubbles, I sailed their boats,
I kept them from each other's throats.
I told them tales of magic lands,
I took them out to wash their hands.
I sorted their rubbers and tied their laces,

I wiped their noses and dried their faces.
Of similarity there's lots
'Twixt tiny tots and Hottentots.
I've earned repose to heal the ravages
Of these angelic-looking savages.
Oh, progeny playing by itself
Is a lonely fascinating elf,
But progeny in roistering dozens
Behaves like boistering blacksheep cousins.
Shunned are the games a parent proposes;
They prefer to squirt each other with hoses,
Their playmates are their natural foemen
And they like to poke each other's abdomen.
Their joy needs another's woe to cushion it
Say a puddle, and somebody littler to push in it.
They observe with glee the ballistic results
Of ice cream with spoons for catapults,
And inform the assembly with tears and glares
That everyone's presents are better than theirs.
Oh, little women and little men,
Someday I hope to love you again,
But not till after the party's over,
So give me the key to the doghouse, Rover.

A LADY THINKS SHE IS THIRTY

Unwillingly Miranda wakes,
Feels the sun with terror,
One unwilling step she takes,
Shuddering to the mirror.

Miranda in Miranda's sight
Is old and gray and dirty;
Twenty-nine she was last night;
This morning she is thirty.

Shining like the morning star,
Like the twilight shining,
Haunted by a calendar,
Miranda sits a-pining.

Silly girl, silver girl,
Draw the mirror toward you;
Time who makes the years to whirl
Adorned as he adored you.

Time is timelessness for you;
Calendars for the human;
What's a year, or thirty, to
Loveliness made woman?

Oh, Night will not see thirty again,
Yet soft her wing, Miranda;
Pick up your glass and tell me, then —
How old is Spring, Miranda?

MR. PEACHEY'S PREDICAMENT
or
NO MOT PARADES

Once there was a man named Mr. Peachey and he lived
on Park Avenue and played the harp and was an
eligible bachelor but his social life was hapless,

And he thought at first it was because his parents came
    from Indianapless,
But one day he awoke from a troubled nap,
And said I am tired of this hapless social life, what I
    want is a social life simply teeming with hap.
It can't be, he said, that I don't play the harp enough,
I wonder if just possibly my wits are not sharp enough.
I know that I'm pretty noted
But I've never been quoted;
Perhaps the solution for me
Is some iridescent repartee;
Suppose before I next dine out I compose a series of
    epigrams of searing astringency
And then I shall be ready with a quip for any conver-
    sational contingency.
So he composed a series of epigrams of indubitable
    variety,
And went to dine with some people way up in soci-
    ety.
And in the taxi he memorized his lines and held a solo
    rehearsal,
And he was delighted, because he said some people's
    humor is specialized but mine is universal.
There may well be a Mr. Shoemaker there who has
    divorced a beautiful rich virtuous wife for a debt-
    ridden hideous wife with a past,
And I'll say Shoemaker you should have stuck to your
    last;
And suppose somebody remarks that the hostess looks
    like a Titian I can bring them up short,
I can answer, Looks like a Titian, eh? Do you mean
    beaut- or mort-?

That will naturally swing the conversation to the books
of Michael Arlen and their merits and faults,
And what do I say then, oh yes, I say I see that Michael
is still dancing to the Merry Ouida waltz,
And I'll go right on and say While we're on the subject
of waltzes I'd like to play a little Haydn for you,
and I'll go to the piano and grope at the keys and
then look up impishly and speak,
And say I really don't know whether I'm playing Haydn
or Haydn seek.
Then after the laughter has died down I shall approach
some Yale man who has just returned from abroad
whom I wish to embarrass
And I'll ask him how he enjoyed the Boola-Boolavards
of Paris.
Oh, said Mr. Peachey gleefully, the days of my hapless
social life are over, I cannot help but be a wow,
I wish I was at the party right now.
But when he got to the party his hostess, who didn't
look like a Titian at all, she looked like a Dali, was
quite sharp,
And sent him right back to his Park Avenue apartment
to get his harp,
And today he is living in the old family mansion in In-
dianapless
Where I'm sorry to say his social life is just as hapless.

NEVERTHELESS

I am not fond of Oliver Montrose.
Oliver is a person I despise;

The purple veins that bulbify his nose,
The crimson veins that irrigate his eyes.
His wheezy breath his vinous weakness shows;
He is the slave of whisky, beer and gin.
I am not fond of Oliver Montrose;
I hate the sinner. But what a warming sin!

Bibesco Poolidge is a man of jowl;
I've never seen a dewlap, but on him;
He shines with the grease of many a basted fowl;
Ten thousand sauces round his innards swim.
The ghosts of hosts of kine about him prowl,
Lamb, pig, and game blood trickles from his chin;
I cannot look on him without a scowl;
I hate the sinner. But what a luscious sin!

I do not dote on Murgatroyd Van Rust,
So tasty to the tenderest of genders.
Practically everything that has a bust
Surveys his suave ensemble and surrenders.
The way he parts his hair I do not trust;
Let the phone ring, I loathe his knowing grin.
You cannot see his diary for the dust,
I hate the sinner. Still, if one had to sin . . .

O Mammonites and spendthrifts, draw ye nigh,
Fingernail-biters and sluggards, come on in,
Consider now how tolerant am I
Who hate the sinner, yet who love the sin.

There is something to be said for the Victorians

Even though they refused to believe they were descended from apes and saurians;

Because take their low opinion of exposure anatomical,

Why I have a feeling that they felt it was not so much immoral as just plain comical.

They realized that most people are big where they should be littler and little where they should be bigger,

And they would rather have had their bathing suit laughed at than their figure.

Yes they wore the costumes they did because they knew that they were not ancient Greeks,

And it is a moot question which is more ludicrous on the beach, the cloistered rompers of 1889, or 1939's ubiquitous physiques.

That belle of the nineties tiptoeing down the steps of the bathing machine may have had the natural lines of a Langtry or again of a prize-winning pumpkin or of a homeless heifer after an extended drought,

But thanks to the marquee enswathing her she got the benefit of the doubt.

Whereas today at Miami or Coney or Catalina,

Why practically everyone is forced to face the fact that their beloved is built like either a flute or a concertina.

I have a theory about physiological disclosures along the strand;

I believe they account for Sally Rand;

I believe that when people have seen a certain number
   of undraped figures like a concertina or a flute,
Well, finally they are willing to pay any amount just
   to see a beaut,
So now it's a hot sultry day and you may all run down to
   the beach for a swim and a look.
I'm going to put on Uncle Elmer's bathing suit and
   sit in the tub and read a Victorian book.

PROCRASTINATION IS ALL OF THE TIME

Torpor and sloth, torpor and sloth,
These are the cooks that unseason the broth.
Slothor and torp, slothor and torp
The directest of bee-line ambitions can warp.
He who is slothic, he who is torporal,
Will not be promoted to sergeant or corporal.
No torporer drowsy, no comatose slother
Will make a good banker, not even an author.
Torpor I deprecate, sloth I deplore,
Torpor is tedious, sloth is a bore.
Sloth is a bore, and torpor is tedious,
Fifty parts comatose, fifty tragedious.
How drear, on a planet redundant with woes,
That sloth is not slumber, nor torpor repose.
That the innocent joy of not getting things done
Simmers sulkily down to plain not having fun.
You smile in the morn like a bride in her bridalness
At the thought of a day of nothing but idleness.
By midday you're slipping, by evening a lunatic,
A perusing-the-newspapers-all-afternoonatic,

Worn to a wraith from the half-hourly jaunt
After glasses of water you didn't want,
And at last when onto your pallet you creep,
You discover yourself too tired to sleep.

O torpor and sloth, torpor and sloth,
These are the cooks that unseason the broth.
Torpor is harrowing, sloth it is irksome —
Everyone ready? Let's go out and worksome.

THE TERRIBLE PEOPLE

People who have what they want are very fond of tell-
    ing people who haven't what they want that they
    really don't want it,
And I wish I could afford to gather all such people into
    a gloomy castle on the Danube and hire half a
    dozen capable Draculas to haunt it.
I don't mind their having a lot of money, and I don't
    care how they employ it,
But I do think that they damn well ought to admit
    they enjoy it.
But no, they insist on being stealthy
About the pleasures of being wealthy,
And the possession of a handsome annuity
Makes them think that to say how hard it is to make
    both ends meet is their bounden duity.
You cannot conceive of an occasion
Which will find them without some suitable evasion.
Yes indeed, with arguments they are very fecund;

Their first point is that money isn't everything, and that
    they have no money anyhow is their second.
Some people's money is merited,
And other people's is inherited,
But wherever it comes from,
They talk about it as if it were something you got pink
    gums from.
This may well be,
But if so, why do they not relieve themselves of the
    burden by transferring it to the deserving poor
    or to me?
Perhaps indeed the possession of wealth is constantly
    distressing,
But I should be quite willing to assume every curse of
    wealth if I could at the same time assume every
    blessing.
The only incurable troubles of the rich are the troubles
    that money can't cure,
Which is a kind of trouble that is even more trouble-
    some if you are poor.
Certainly there are lots of things in life that money
    won't buy, but it's very funny —
Have you ever tried to buy them without money?

SONG FOR THE SADDEST IDES

Hayfoot, strawfoot, forward march!
Stiffen your backbone up with starch!
Strut like Hercules or Hector!
Ready for the Income Tax Collector!

Give three cheers and give them thrice!
Roar like lions, or maybe mice!
Rush like lightning, or maybe glue,
To the Dept. of Internal Revenue.

Left foot, right foot, heel and toe,
One little drink and off we go,
Fresh from the tub in our Sunday raiment,
Wee hands clutching the quarterly payment.

Citizen? Resident? Married? Single?
Living together, or don't you mingle?
Blessed events? If so, please state
Change of status, its nature and date.

Royalties? Rents? Commissions? Fees?
If none, explain their absence, please.
And let there be no legal flaw
In Deductions Authorized by Law.

Salaries? Wages? Sale of Property?
Here comes the Notary, hippety-hoppety!
Raise your hand and take your oath
To tell the truth or bust. Or both.

Boomelay boom on the big bass drum!
Where is the money coming from?
You must borrow and I must beg,
And the last to pay is a rotten egg.

Presto! Changeo! Hullabaloo!
Where does the money vanish to?

It's used in research, children dear,
For ways to increase the tax next year.

THE ROOSTER

The rooster has a soul more bellicose
Than all your Ludendorffs and Jellicoes.
His step is prouder than Davy Crockett's,
As he swaggers by with his hands in his pockets.

HUSH, HERE THEY COME

Some people get savage and bitter when to backbiters
they refer,
But I just purr.
Yes, some people consider backbiters to be rankest of
the rank,
But frankly, I prefer them to people who go around being frank,
Because usually when you are backbitten behind your
back you don't know about it and it doesn't leave
a trace,
But frankness consists of having your back bitten right
to your face,
And as if that weren't enough to scar you,
Why you are right there in person to scotch the def-
amation, and if you don't happen to be able to
scotch it, why where are you?
Frank people are grim, but genuine backbiters are delightful to have around,

Because they are so anxious that if what they have
    been saying about you has reached your ears you
    shouldn't believe it, that they are the most amiable
    companions to be found;
They will entertain you from sunset to dawn,
And cater encouragingly to all your weaknesses so that
    they can broadcast them later on,
So what if they do gnaw on your spine after enjoying
    your beer and skittles?
I don't blame them the least of jots or tittles,
Because certainly no pastime such diversion lends
As talking friends over analytically with friends,
So what if as they leave your house or you leave theirs
    backbiters strip your flesh and your clothes off,
At least it is your back that they bite, and not your nose
    off.
I believe in a place for everything and everything in its
    place,
And I don't care how unkind the things people say
    about me so long as they don't say them to my
    face.

THE FACTS OF LIFE

Daughter, dim those reverent eyes;
Daddy must apologize.
Daddy's not an engineer;
Never will be, now, I fear.
Daddy couldn't drive a train,
Not for all the sherry in Spain.

Daddy's not a fireman, too;
He couldn't do what firemen do.
Clanging bells and screaming sirens
Are no part of his environs.
In case of fire, no hero he;
Merely a humble rescuee.

Also, greatly to his grief,
Daddy's not an Indian chief.
Daddy cannot stealthy walk
Or wield a lethal tomahawk.
Hark to Daddy's secret grim:
Feathers only tickle him.

Better learn it now than later:
Daddy's not an aviator.
Daddy cannot soar and swoop,
Neither can he loop the loop.
Parachutes he never hung on to,
And what is worse, he doesn't want to.

As long as Daddy's being defiant,
Daddy, child, is not a giant.
You'll travel far if you would seek
A less remarkable physique.
That's why he feels a decade older
When you are riding on his shoulder.

Another thing that Daddy ain't,
I frankly tell you, is a saint.
Daddy, my faithful catechumen,
Is widely known as all too human.

Still, if you watch him, you will find
He does his best, when so inclined.

One final skeleton while I dare:
Daddy's not a millionaire.
Alas, his most amusing verse
Is not a Fortunatus purse.
What I should buy for you, my sweeting,
Did journals end in both ends meeting!

There, child, you have the dismal truth,
Now obvious as an absent tooth.
Your doom it is to be the daughter
Of one as flat as barley water.
Do you mind so much, since he was made so?
What's that, my own? . . . I was afraid so.

A RIDE ON THE BRONXIAL LOCAL

So this is bronchitis.
Well at least it is not appendicitis.
Well I suppose I ought to be thankful it's not bubonic
    or pellagra.
Well I suppose I ought to be thankful I'm having it in
    bed instead of floating in a barrel over Niagra,
And that is about all that can be said for it,
Particularly when you try to sustain life on what you get
    fed for it,
And you drink water, water, water, and the only other
    ingredient in it is sometimes soda and sometimes
    aspirin,

And when your helpmeet approaches to help, you are
very grateful but you are afraid of giving her what
you have got, and a grateful embrace is the last
thing you can claspirin,
And if you smoke you increase your cough
But finally you decide you'd rather increase it than
lay off,
And sometimes you are cold and that's a chill and
sometimes you are hot and that's a fever
And all in all you are as merry as Danny Deever.
And if you try to read you go to sleep and if you go
to sleep you are waked up by somebody advancing
on your bedside without any stealth
And they poke a spoonful of something at you and tell
you to swallow it and regain your health
And then you decide that if that is the only way to
regain your health you just don't want to,
And then you begin to wonder who gave you your
beautiful bonny bronchitis, and then finally you
get to the fun of thinking who it would be fun to
pass it on to,
And first of all for the good of humanity,
You'd like to give it to all dictators and political spell-
binders of dubious sanity,
Because if they had bronchitis they couldn't spellbind
and if they couldn't spellbind they couldn't dictate, and if they couldn't dictate they would have
to stop going around with their jaws out or their
right hands raised or their arms akimbo,
And they would sink back into their original limbo.
And something I should love even better than possums
love persimmons

Would be to hand on my bronchitis to all singers who
    if they are women have voices like men's and if
    they are men have voices like women's,
And then, except for the sound of coughing, the day
    and night air would be quiet as it was before the
    birth of Marconi or Edison,
And now good-by thank you because I must explain to
    a woman that I don't need any more medicine.

THE TURTLE

The turtle lives 'twixt plated decks
Which practically conceal its sex.
I think it clever of the turtle
In such a fix to be so fertile.

IT'S NEVER FAIR WEATHER

I do not like the winter wind
That whistles from the North.
My upper teeth and those beneath,
They jitter back and forth.
Oh, some are hanged, and some are skinned,
And others face the winter wind.

I do not like the summer sun
That scorches the horizon.
Though some delight in Fahrenheit,
To me it's deadly pizen.

I think that life would be more fun
Without the simmering summer sun.

I do not like the signs of spring,
The fever and the chills,
The icy mud, the puny bud,
The frozen daffodils.
Let other poets gayly sing;
I do not like the signs of spring.

I do not like the foggy fall
That strips the maples bare;
The radiator's mating call,
The dank, rheumatic air.
I fear that taken all in all,
I do not like the foggy fall.

The winter sun is always kind,
And summer wind's a savior,
And I'll merrily sing of fall and spring
When they're on their good behavior.
But otherwise I see no reason
To speak in praise of any season.

DON'T GRIN, OR YOU'LL HAVE TO
BEAR IT

It is better in the long run to possess an abscess or a
  tumor
Than to possess a sense of humor.

People who have senses of humor have a very good
    time,
But they never accomplish anything of note, either
    despicable or sublime,
Because how can anybody accomplish anything im-
    mortal
When they realize they look pretty funny doing it and
    have to stop to chortle?
Everybody admits that Michelangelo's little things in
    the Sistine Chapel are so immortal they have
    everybody reeling,
But I'll bet he could never have dashed them off if
    he had realized how undignified he looked lying
    up there with his stomach on the ceiling.
Do you think Der Führer could keep on being Der
    Führer
If he saw what everybody else sees every time he looks
    in the mührer?
Yes, fatal handicaps in life are fortunately few,
But the most fatal of all is the faculty of seeing the
    other person's point of view,
And if your devoted mother suggests that you will some
    day be rich and famous, why perish the suggestion;
That is, perish it if you are afflicted with the suspicion
    that there are two sides to every question.
Good gracious, how could anybody corner wheat
If they were sissy enough to reflect that they were caus-
    ing a lot of other people to be unable to afford
    to eat?
Look at mayors and congressmen and presidents, always
    excepting college presidents, such as Harvard's
    Conant;

Do you think they could get elected if they admitted
  even to themselves that there was anything to be
  said for their opponent?
No, no, genius won't get you as far as common every-
  day facility
Unless it is accompanied by a conviction of infallibility,
And people who have a sense of humor are extremely
  gullible,
But not enough so, alas, to believe that they are in-
  fullible.

ISN'T THAT A DAINTY DISH? NO!

I am tired of gadgets with cocktails,
I am awfully tired of gadgets with cocktails,
My heart leaps down when I behold gadgets with cock-
  tails,
With me they have outlived their popularity.
Gadgets with cocktails are stultified,
Gadgets with cocktails are stertorous,
Gadgets with cocktails are stark and stagnant,
And for them I have no patience or charity.

I don't want any toast covered with vulcanized caviar,
Or any soggy popcorn covered with cheesy butter or
  buttery cheese,
I don't want any potato chips or Tiny Tootsie pretzels
  or pretzel sticks,
And I don't want any crackers coated with meat paste
  or bargain pâté de foie gras particularly, please.

Do not hand me that plate filled with olives unripe and
    overripe,
Anchovies whether curled or uncurled I have concluded
    not to abide,
Kindly mail all those salted peanuts and almonds to
    the Collector of Internal Revenue,
As well as all the little heart-shaped sandwiches filled
    with squashy stuff that when you pick them up
    they squirt out at the side.

Maybe somewhere there is somebody who would like
    the stuffed eggs and diminutive frankfurters,
Or who could look the stuffed celery in the eye and
    voluntarily chew it,
Maybe there is a Chinaman in China who would care
    for that slab of fumigated salmon,
And that thing whatever it is all rolled up with a tooth-
    pick sticking through it.

Hostesses never tire of gadgets with cocktails,
Hostesses sit around thinking up new gadgets with
    cocktails,
They prowl through the papers hunting tricky gadgets
    for cocktails,
And if they don't serve more than other hostesses they
    are swamped with humiliation and grief;
Gadgets with cocktails to you, my dear Mrs. Marsh-
    mallow,
Gadgets with cocktails to you, Mrs. Rodney St. Rodney,
Gadgets with cocktails to you and all other hostesses,
And I'll take some bread and butter and a slice of rare
    roast beef.

There are some people of whom I would certainly like
    to be one,
Who are the people who get things done.
They never forget to send their evening shirts to the
    laundry and then when they need them can't find
    anything but a lot of shirts without any starch,
And they always file their income tax return by the
    fourteenth of March.
They balance their checkbooks every month and their
    figures always agree with the bank's,
And they are prompt in writing letters of condolence
    or thanks.
They never leave anything to chance,
But always make reservations in advance.
When they get out of bed they never neglect to don
    slippers so they never pick up athlete's foot or a
    cold or a splinter,
And they hang their clothes up on hangers every night
    and put their winter clothes away every summer
    and their summer clothes away every winter.
Before spending any money they insist on getting an
    estimate or a sample,
And if they lose anything from a shoelace to a diamond
    ring it is covered by insurance more than ample.
They have budgets and what is more they live inside of
    them,
Even though it means eating things made by recipes
    clipped from the Sunday paper that you'd think
    they would have died of them.
They serve on committees

And improve their cities.

They are modern knight-errants

Who remember their godchildren's birthdays and the anniversaries of their godchildren's parents,

And in cold weather they remember the birds and supply them with sunflower seed and suet,

And whatever they decide to do, whether it's to save twenty-five per cent of their salary or learn Italian or write a musical comedy or touch their toes a hundred times every morning before breakfast, why they go ahead and do it.

People who get things done lead contented lives, or at least I guess so,

And I certainly wish that either I were more like them or they were less so.

IT MUST BE THE MILK

There is a thought that I have tried not to but cannot help but think,

Which is, My goodness how much infants resemble people who have had quite a bit too much to drink.

Tots,

Sots;

So different and yet so identical!

What a humiliating coincidence for pride parentical!

Yet when you see your little dumpling set sail across the nursery floor,

Can you conscientiously deny the resemblance to some-

body who is leaving a tavern after having tried to
leave it a dozen times and each time turned back
for just one more?

Each step achieved

Is simply too good to be believed;

Foot somehow follows foot

And somehow manages to stay put;

Arms wildly semaphore,

Wild eyes seem to ask, Whatever did we get in such
a dilemma for?

Doggedly they pursue their course,

Which is as devious as testimony in a contested divorce,

And their gait is more that of a duckling than a Greek
goddessling or godling,

And in inebriates it's called staggering but in infants
it's called toddling.

Another kinship with topers is also by infants exhibited,

Which is that they are completely uninhibited,

And they can't talk straight

Any more than they can walk straight;

Their pronunciation is awful

And their grammar is flawful,

And in adults it's maudlin and deplorable,

But in infants it's tunnin' and adorable,

So I hope you will agree that it is very hard to tell an
infant from somebody who has gazed too long into
the cup,

And really the only way you can tell them apart is to
wait till next day, and the infant is the one that
feels all right when it wakes up.

THE FISH

The fish, when he's exposed to air,
Can show no trace of savoir faire,
But in the sea regains his balance
And exploits all his manly talents.
The chastest of the vertebrates,
He never even sees his mates,
But when they've finished, he appears
And O.K.'s all their bright ideas.

DON'T GUESS, LET ME TELL YOU

Personally I don't care whether a detective story writer
    was educated in night school or day school
So long as they don't belong to the H.I.B.K. school.
The H.I.B.K. being a device to which too many detec-
    tive story writers are prone,
Namely the Had I But Known.
Sometimes it is the Had I But Known what grim secret
    lurked behind that smiling exterior I would never
    have set foot within the door,
Sometimes the Had I But Known then what I know
    now I could have saved at least three lives by re-
    vealing to the Inspector the conversation I heard
    through that fortuitous hole in the floor.
Had-I-But-Known narrators are the ones who hear a
    stealthy creak at midnight in the tower where the
    body lies, and, instead of locking their door or
    arousing the drowsy policeman posted outside their
    room, sneak off by themselves to the tower and

suddenly they hear a breath exhaled behind them,
And they have no time to scream, they know nothing
else till the men from the D.A.'s office come in
next morning and find them.
Had I But Known-ers are quick to assume the preroga-
tives of the Deity,
For they will suppress evidence that doesn't suit their
theories with appalling spontaneity,
And when the killer is finally trapped into a confession
by some elaborate device of the Had I But Known-
er some hundred pages later than if they hadn't
held their knowledge aloof,
Why they say Why Inspector I knew all along it was
he but I couldn't tell you, you would have laughed
at me unless I had absolute proof.
Would you like a nice detective story for your library
which I am sorry to say I didn't rent but owns?
I wouldn't have bought it had I but known it was
impregnated with Had I But Knowns.

THE SECRET TOWN

There is a town within a town,
Where my true love walks alone,
And green, oh, meadow green, is her gown,
And daffodil gold her shoon.

Unto that silent, secret place,
No street, no alley, leads.
A town without a market place,
No huckster crowd it feeds.

The wagon wheels without the wall,
They are not heard within.
The angry bells that clash and call,
They may not enter in.

And thunderheads their thunder lose;
Such is the stillness there,
That in the grassy avenues
The deer feeds, and the hare.

And there the hot sun softlier sifts,
And the harsh wind softlier blows,
And the frost melts, and the fog lifts,
And earlier springs the rose.

Within that town a lady walks
In dear serenity,
And lilies on their slender stalks
Less stately are than she.

Less delicate the violets are,
Less light of foot the deer,
Less lovely is the evening star,
Than she who walketh here.

I built that greedy outer town,
And she the town within.
When my own creature howls me down,
She bids me enter in.

Oh meadow, meadow green is her gown,
And daffodil gold her shoon.

God keep the town within a town,
Where my true love walks alone.

MAN BITES DOG–DAYS

In this fairly temperate clime
Summertime is itchy time.
O'er rocks and stumps and ruined walls
Shiny poison ivy crawls.
Every walk in woods and fields
Its aftermath of itching yields.
Hand me down my rusty hatchet;
Someone murmured, Do not scratch it.

Reason permeates my rhyme:
Summertime is itchy time.
Beneath the orange August moon
Overfed mosquitoes croon.
After sun-up, flies and midges
Raise on people bumps and ridges.
Hand me down my rusty hatchet;
Someone murmured, Do not scratch it.

Lo, the year is in its prime;
Summertime is itchy time.
People loll upon the beaches
Ripening like gaudy peaches.
Friends, the beach is not the orchard,
Nor is the peach by sunburn tortured.
Hand me down my rusty hatchet;
Someone murmured, Do not scratch it.

Now the menu is sublime;
Summertime is itchy time.
Berries, clams, and lobsters tease
Our individual allergies.
Rash in rosy splendor thrives,
Running neck-and-neck with hives.
Hand me down my rusty hatchet;
Someone murmured, Do not scratch it.

The bluebells and the cowbells chime;
Summertime is itchy time.
Despite cold soup, and ice, and thermoses,
Garments cling to epidermises.
That fiery-footed centipede,
Prickly Heat, prowls forth to feed.
Hand me down my rusty hatchet;
Someone murmured, Do not scratch it.

Hatchet-killings ain't a crime:
Summertime is itchy time.

POOR MR. STRAWBRIDGE

Once there was a man named Mr. Strawbridge,
And all he wanted was a drawbridge,
But when people asked him what kind
He couldn't make up his mind.
His fingernails he would bite and his thumbs he would
    twiddle
Trying to decide whether he wanted one that revolved
    on a pivot or one that went up in the middle,

So finally everybody went to Mr. Strawbridge
And asked him why he wanted a drawbridge.
And Mr. Strawbridge smiled a smile seraphic
And said he wanted it because he wanted to interfere
     with traffic.
He said it gave him great satisfaction
To sit on his veranda and watch the Atlantic Ocean in
     action
But he said sometimes on Sundays and holidays he
     couldn't see the Altantic for the motorists,
And he said he'd rather see the former than the latter
     even though they were handsome and respectable
     Kiwanians and Lions and Rotarists,
And he said maybe he was a silly old goose,
But it always gave him a pain to see a line of auto-
     mobiles practically hooked up together like freight
     cars on a long freight train, particularly when the
     freight train was ten miles long and you never
     seemed to get to the caboose,
And he said that doubtless all that gipsying was most
     romantic,
But he still preferred looking at the Atlantic,
And he said he didn't see why people went out in one
     automobile between a lot of other automobiles,
     because they didn't get any air or scenery,
No, they just got a view of the license plate in front
     and a lot of annoyance and dust and gasolinery,
And therefore, said Mr. Strawbridge,
Everybody else would see just as much and I would
     see much more if they were all held up somewhere
     by an open drawbridge,
So all his friends said he was a genius,

And they gave him a lot of orchids and gardenius,
But they never gave him a drawbridge,
And that is why I call him poor Mr. Strawbridge.

A WATCHED EXAMPLE NEVER BOILS

The weather is so very mild
That some would call it warm.
Good gracious, aren't we lucky, child?
Here comes a thunderstorm.

The sky is now indelible ink,
The branches reft asunder;
But you and I, we do not shrink;
We love the lovely thunder.

The garden is a raging sea,
The hurricane is snarling;
Oh happy you and happy me!
Isn't the lightning darling?

Fear not the thunder, little one.
It's weather, simply weather;
It's friendly giants full of fun
Clapping their hands together.

I hope of lightning our supply
Will never be exhausted;
You know it's lanterns in the sky
For angels who are losted.

We love the kindly wind and hail,
The jolly thunderbolt,
We watch in glee the fairy trail
Of ampere, watt, and volt.

Oh, than to enjoy a storm like this
There's nothing I would rather.
Don't dive beneath the blankets, Miss!
Or else leave room for Father.

THE STRANGE CASE OF THE IRKSOME PRUDE

Once upon a time there was a young man named
Harold Scrutiny.

ɔↄ

Harold had many virtues and practically no vices.

ɔↄ

He smoked, to be sure.

ɔↄ

Also he drank and swore.

ɔↄ

Moreover, he was a pickpocket.

ɔↄ

But, for all that, Harold was no prude.

ɔↄ

I am no prude, Harold often said.

ɔↄ

But Detective Guilfoyle of the Pickpocket Squad is a
prude, the old prude, said Harold.

ɔↄ

One day Harold went into the subway to pick some
   pockets.

∽

There was a man on the platform penciling a beard on
   the lady on the toothpaste placard.

∽

Hey, said Harold.

∽

Hey who, said the man.

∽

Hey you, that's hey who, said Harold.

∽

Aren't you going to give her a mustache?

∽

Sure I'm going to give her a mustache, said the man.

∽

What do you think I am?

∽

I think you're somebody that puts the beard on ladies
   on toothpaste placards before they put on the mustache, said Harold.

∽

Don't you know enough to put the mustache on first?

∽

You put the mustache on first, why then you can turn
   it up or turn it down, whichever you want, said
   Harold.

∽

You try to turn a mustache down after the beard's on,
   it runs into the beard, said Harold.

∽

It don't look like a mustache, only like a beard grows up and down both.

∽

Go on, said the man, go on and pick some pockets.

∽

Harold turned to his work, but his mind was elsewhere.

∽

Suddenly the lady on the toothpaste placard got off the toothpaste placard and arrested him.

∽

It was Detective Guilfoyle of the Pickpocket Squad all the time.

∽

You got a beard grows up and down both, said Harold.

∽

Detective Guilfoyle searched Harold.

∽

He certainly was surprised at what he found.

∽

So was Harold.

∽

Harold hadn't picked any pockets at all because his mind was elsewhere.

∽

He had picked a peck of pickled peppers.

∽

Detective Guilfoyle wanted to call Harold a name, but he couldn't because he was a prude.

∽

Harold picked his pocket and later became the smokingest, swearingest, drinkingest Assistant District Attorney the county ever had.

∽

Don't be a prude.

· 57 ·

BIOLOGICAL REFLECTION

A girl whose cheeks are covered with paint
Has an advantage with me over one whose ain't.

WHEN THE DEVIL WAS SICK COULD
HE PROVE IT?

Few things are duller
Than feeling unspecifically off-color,
Yes, you feel like the fulfilment of a dismal prophecy,
And you don't feel either exercisey or officey,
But still you can't produce a red throat or a white
    tongue or uneasy respiration or any kind of a
    symptom,
And it is very embarrassing that whoever was supposed
    to be passing out the symptoms skympton,
Because whatever is the matter with you, you can't
    spot it
But whatever it is, you've got it,
But the question is how to prove it,
And you suck for hours on the mercury of the ther-
    mometer you finally sent out for and you can't
    move it,
And your entire system may be pneumococci'd or
    streptococci'd,
But the looks you get from your loved ones are simply
    skepticocci'd,
And Conscience, that thin-lipped prude, raises her
    vaunted haunted to-do,
Crying There's nothing the matter with you, you're

just trying to get out of doing something you never
wanted to do;
So you unfinger your pulse before Conscience can jeer
at you for a fingerer,
And you begin to believe that perhaps she is right, per-
haps you are nothing but a hypochondriacal old
malingerer,
And you take a farewell look at the thermometer,
And that's when you hurl the bometer.
Yes sir, it's as good as a tonic,
Because you've got as pretty a ninety-nine point one as
you'd wish to see in a month of bubonic.
Some people hold out for a hundred or more before
they collapse
But that leaves too many gaps;
As for me,
I can get a very smug Monday Tuesday Wednesday
Thursday or Friday in bed out of a tenth of a de-
gree.
It is to this trait that I am debtor
For the happy fact that on week ends I generally feel
better.

SPRING SONG

Listen, buds, it's March twenty-first;
Don't you know enough to burst?
Come on, birds, unlock your throats!
Come on, gardeners, shed your coats!
Come on zephyrs, come on flowers,
Come on grass, and violet showers!

And come on, lambs, in frisking flocks!
Salute the vernal equinox!
Twang the cheerful lute and zither!
Spring is absolutely hither!
Yester eve was dark despair,
With winter, winter, everywhere;
Today, upon the other hand,
'Tis spring throughout this happy land.
Oh, such is Nature's chiaroscuro,
According to the Weather Bureau.

Then giddy-ap, Napoleon! Giddy-ap, Gideon!
The sun has crossed the right meridian!
What though the blasts of winter sting?
Officially, at least, it's spring,
And be it far from our desire
To make the Weather Man a liar!

So, blossom, ye parks, with cozy benches,
Occupied by blushing wenches!
Pipe, ye frogs, while swains are sighing,
And furnaces unwept are dying!
Crow, ye cocks, a little bit louder!
Mount, ye sales of paint and powder!
Croon, ye crooner, yet more croonishly!
Shine, ye moon, a lot more moonishly!
And O ye brooklets, burst your channels!
And O ye camphor, greet ye flannels!
And bloom, ye clothesline, bloom with wash,
Where erstwhile squudged the grim galosh!
Ye transit lines abet our follies
By turning loose your open trolleys!

And ye, ye waking hibernators,
Drain Anti-freeze from your radiators!
While ye, ye otherwise useless dove,
Remember, please, to rhyme with love.

Then giddy-ap, Napoleon! Giddy-ap, Gideon!
The sun has crossed the right meridian!
What though the blasts of winter sting?
Officially, at least, it's spring!

THE SHREW

Strange as it seems, the smallest mammal
Is the shrew, and not the camel.
And that is all I ever knew,
Or wish to know, about the shrew.

WILL CONSIDER SITUATION

These here are words of radical advice for a young man
    looking for a job:
Young man, be a snob.
Yes, if you are in search of arguments against starting
    at the bottom,
Why I've gottom.
Let the personnel managers differ;
It's obvious that you will get on faster at the top than
    at the bottom because there are more people at the
    bottom than at the top so naturally the competi-
    tion at the bottom is stiffer.

If you need any further proof that my theory works,

Well, nobody can deny that presidents get paid more
than vice-presidents and vice-presidents get paid
more than clerks.

Stop looking at me quizzically;

I want to add that you will never achieve fortune in
a job that makes you uncomfortable physically.

When anybody tells you that hard jobs are better for
you than soft jobs be sure to repeat this text to
them,

Postmen tramp around all day through rain and snow
just to deliver people in cozy air-conditioned offices
checks to them.

You don't need to interpret tea leaves stuck in a cup

To understand that people who work sitting down get
paid more than people who work standing up.

Another thing about having a comfortable job is you
not only accumulate more treasure;

You get more leisure.

So that when you find you have worked so comfortably
that your waistline is a menace,

You correct it with golf or tennis.

Whereas if in an uncomfortable job like piano-moving
or stevedoring you indulge,

You have no time for exercise, you just continue to
bulge.

To sum it up, young man, there is every reason to refuse a job that will make heavy demands on you
corporally or manually,

And the only intelligent way to start your career is to
accept a sitting position paying at least twenty-five
thousand dollars annually.

PRAYER AT THE END OF A ROPE

Dear Lord, observe this bended knee,
This visage meek and humble,
And heed this confidential plea,
Voiced in a reverent mumble.

I ask no miracles or stunts,
No heavenly radiogram;
I only beg for once, just once,
To not be in a jam.

One little moment thy servant craves
Of being his own master;
One placid vale between the waves
Of duty and disaster.

Oh, when the postman's whistle shrills,
Just once, Lord, let me grin;
Let me have settled last month's bills
Before this month's come in.

Let me not bite more off the cob
Than I have teeth to chew;
Please let me finish just one job
Before the next is due.

Consider, too, my social life,
Sporadic though it be;
Why is it only mental strife
That pleasure brings to me?

For months, when people entertain,
Me they do not invite;

Then suddenly invitations rain,
All for the self-same night.

R.S.V.P.'s I pray thee send
Alone and not in bunches,
Or teach me I cannot attend
Two dinners or two lunches.

Let me my hostess not insult,
Not call her diamonds topaz;
Else harden me to the result
Of my fantastic faux pas.

One little lull, Lord, that's my plea,
Then loose the storm again;
Just once, this once, I beg to be
Not in a jam. Amen.

THE PANTHER

The panther is like a leopard,
Except it hasn't been peppered.
Should you behold a panther crouch,
Prepare to say Ouch.
Better yet, if called by a panther,
Don't anther.

GOLLY, HOW TRUTH WILL OUT!

How does a person get to be a capable liar?
That is something that I respectfully inquiar,

Because I don't believe a person will ever set the
    world on fire
Unless they are a capable lire.
Some wise man said that words were given to us to con-
    ceal our thoughts,
But if a person has nothing but truthful words why
    their thoughts haven't even the protection of a
    pair of panties or shoughts,
And a naked thought is ineffectual as well as improper,
And hasn't a chance in the presence of a glib chinchilla-
    clad whopper.
One of the greatest abilities a person can have, I guess,
Is the ability to say Yes when they mean No and No
    when they mean Yes.
Oh to be Machiavellian, oh to be unscrupulous, oh, to
    be glib!
Oh to be ever prepared with a plausible fib!
Because then a dinner engagement or a contract or a
    treaty is no longer a fetter,
Because liars can just logically lie their way out of it
    if they don't like it or if one comes along that they
    like better;
And do you think their conscience prickles?
No, it tickles.
And please believe that I mean every one of these lines
    as I am writing them
Because once there was a small boy who was sent to the
    drugstore to buy some bitter stuff to put on his
    nails to keep him from biting them,
And in his humiliation he tried to lie to the clerk
And it didn't work,
Because he said My mother sent me to buy some bitter

stuff for a friend of mine's nails that bites them, and the clerk smiled wisely and said I wonder who that friend could be,

And the small boy broke down and said Me,

And it was me, or at least I was him,

And all my subsequent attempts at subterfuge have been equally grim,

And that is why I admire a suave prevarication because I prevaricate so awkwardly and gauchely,

And that is why I can never amount to anything politically or socially.

DID SOMEONE SAY "BABIES"?

Everybody who has a baby thinks everybody who hasn't a baby ought to have a baby,

Which accounts for the success of such plays as the Irish Rose of Abie,

The idea apparently being that just by being fruitful

You are doing something beautiful,

Which if it is true

Means that the common housefly is several million times more beautiful than me or you.

Also, everybody who hasn't a baby thinks it correct to give tongue

To ecstatic phrases and clauses at the sight of other people's young.

Who is responsible for this propaganda that fills all our houses from their attics to their kitchens?

Is it the perambulator trust or the safety pin manufacturers or the census takers or the obstetritchens?

Why do we continue not only to be hoodwinked by
    them but even lend ourselves to furthering their
    plots
By all the time talking about how nice it is to have a
    houseful of tots?
Men and women everywhere would have a lot more
    chance of acquiring recreation and fame and finan-
    cial independence
If they didn't have to spend most of their time and
    money tending and supporting two or three unat-
    tractive descendants.
We could soon upset this kettle of fish, forsooth,
If every adult would only come out and tell every other
    adult the truth.
To arms, adults! Kindle the beacon fires!
Women, do you want to be nothing but dams? Men,
    do you want to be nothing but sires?
To arms, Mr. President! Call out the army, the navy,
    the marines, the militia, the cadets and the mid-
    dies.
Down with the kiddies!

OUT IS OUT

Come in, dear guests, we've got a treat for you,
We've prepared a different place to eat for you!
Guess where we're going to have our dinner!
Everyone guess! Who'll be the winner?
The dining room? Heavens! It's hereby stated
That dining rooms are dreadfully dated.
What in the world could be more plebeian

Than to eat in a place in which you can see in!
The living room? No, you're off the path;
No, not the bedroom; no, not the bath;
And not the cellar; and not the attic;
The kitchen? No, that's too democratic.
Do you all give up? Well, listen and hark:
We're going to dine outdoors, in the dark!
We're going to dine outdoors, on the terrace,
As dark as an Anti-kink heir or heiress.
No lights, because there aren't any plugs,
And anyhow, lights attract the bugs,
And anyhow, in the dark we've found
There are bugs enough to go around.
Oh, it's drizzling a little; I think perhaps
The girls had better keep on their wraps;
Just strike a match and enjoy the way
The raindrops splash in the consommé.
You probably won't get botts or pellagra
From whatever lit on your pâté de foie gras.
Now, you're not expected to eat with skill,
And everybody's supposed to spill;
If your half-broiled chicken leaps about,
That's half the excitement of eating out;
If you dust it with sugar instead of salt,
It's everyone's fun and nobody's fault;
And if anything flies in your mouth, perchance,
Why, that is mystery, that's romance!
Such a frolic and such a lark
It is to eat outdoors in the dark!
The dandiest fun since I don't know when;
Would you eat in a stuffy old room again?
Oh yes you would, you lukewarm liars,
And I'll see you tomorrow at the cleaner's and dyer's.

THE SQUIRREL

A squirrel to some is a squirrel,
To others, a squirrel's a squirl.
Since freedom of speech is the birthright of each,
I can only this fable unfurl:
A virile young squirrel named Cyril,
In an argument over a girl,
Was lambasted from here to the Tyrol
By a churl of a squirl named Earl.

HOW LONG HAS THIS BEEN GOING ON?
OH, QUITE LONG

Some people think that they can beat three two's with
    a pair of aces,
And other people think they can wind up ahead of the
    races,
And lest we forget,
The people who think they can wind up ahead of the
    races are everybody who has ever won a bet.
Yes, when you first get back five-sixty for two, oh what
    a rosy-toed future before you looms,
But actually your doom is sealed by whoever it is that
    goes around sealing people's dooms,
And you are lost forever
Because you think you won not because you were lucky
    but because you were clever.
You think the race ended as it did, not because you
    hoped it,
But because you doped it,

And from then on you withdraw your savings from the
    bank in ever-waxing wads

Because you are convinced that having figured out one
    winner you can figure out many other winners at
    even more impressive odds,

And pretty soon overdrawing your account or not bet-
    ting at all is the dilemma which you are betwixt

And certainly you're not going to not bet at all because
    you are sure you will eventually wind up ahead be-
    cause the only reason the races haven't run true to
    form, by which you mean your form, is because
    they have been fixed,

So all you need to be a heavy gainer

Is to bet on one honest race or make friends with one
    dishonest trainer.

And I don't know for which this situation is worse,

Your character or your purse.

I don't say that race-tracks are centers of sin,

I only say that they are only safe to go to as long as you
    fail to begin to win.

WASHINGTON'S BIRTHDAY EVE

George Washington was a gentleman,
A soldier and a scholar;
He crossed the Delaware with a boat;
The Potomac *, with a dollar.
The British faced him full of joy,
And departed full of sorrow;

* Sometimes spelled Rappahannock.

George Washington was a gentleman.
His birthday is tomorrow.

When approached by fellow patriots,
And asked for his opinion,
He spoke in accents clear and bold,
And, probably, Virginian.
His winter home at Valley Forge
Was underheated, rather.
He possessed a sturdy Roman nose,
And became his country's father.

His army was a hungry horde,
Ill-armed, worse-clad Colonials;
He was our leading President,
And discouraged ceremonials.
His portrait on our postage stamps,
It does him less than justice;
He was much respected by his wife,
The former Mrs. Custis.

He built and launched our Ship of State,
He brought it safe to harbor;
He wore no beard upon his chin,
Thanks to his faithful barber.
And so my dears, his grateful land
In robes of glory clad him.
George Washington was a gentleman.
I'm glad his parents had him.

THE KITTEN

The trouble with a kitten is
THAT
Eventually it becomes a
CAT.

FOR THE MOST IMPROBABLE SHE

What shall I do with So-and-So?
She won't say Yes and she won't say No.
She tiptoes around the cunningest traps
With a smile and a murmur of Perhaps.
At nine I'm Darling, at ten I'm You —
Tell me, what is a man to do
When the lady his life is based upon
Likes to be wooed but won't be won?

What shall I do with So-and-So?
She won't say Come and she won't say Go.
I'm on my way, but I don't know where —
I wouldn't care, if I didn't care.
Damn the man who invented the story
That a little suspense is salutory.
I swear, by lipstick and powder puff,
Fun is fun, but enough's enough!

What shall I do with So-and-So?
She confesses that I am her favorite beau;
But let the topic of marriage arise
And see the astonishment in her eyes!

Why am I chosen so to be harried?
Other people have gotten married.
Is every courtship conducted thus
Or is it only confined to us?

What shall I do with So-and-So?
If it isn't Yes it must be No,
But who so apathetic as me
To all the other fish in the sea?
On the other hand there's the other guess —
If it isn't No it must be Yes.
In fact, my own, I so adore you
I'm willing to give your answer for you.

I KNOW YOU'LL LIKE THEM

You don't need to study any ponderous tome
To find out how to make your out-of-town guests feel
        not at home,
Because there is one way which couldn't be exquisiter
For enthralling the visitor.
You plan a little gathering informal and sociable
And you ask a few friends whose manners are irre-
        proaciable,
And you speak up with all the pride of Mr. Dewey an-
        nouncing a couple of important impending arrests,
And you say Friends, this is Mr. and Mrs. Comfit-
        monger, my out-of-town guests,
And you even amplify your introduction so as to break
        the ice with more velocity,

And you tell them that Mrs. Comfitmonger used to be
a policewoman and Mr. Comfitmonger is a piano
tuner of no mean virtuosity,

And you hint that Mr. Comfitmonger has had some
pretty intriguing experiences in his years as a vir-
tuoso,

And that Mrs. Comfitmonger while pounding her beat
has dealt with personalities who would scare the
pants off Lombroso,

And that everything is all set for a dandy evening of
general chitchat is what you think,

And you retire to the pantry to prepare everybody a
drink,

And you hear the brouhaha of vivacious voices,

And your heart rejoices,

Because it seems that your friends find Mr. Comfitmonger's anecdotes of life under the Steinways fascinating,

And are spellbound by Mrs. Comfitmonger's articulate
opposition to arson and assassinating,

And you say This party is indeed de luxe,

And you emerge to find all your friends excitedly dis-
cussing putts that wouldn't go down and stocks
that wouldn't go up, and Mr. and Mrs. Comfitmonger over in a corner leafing through your
books,

And if you think you can turn the conversation to Pa-
lestrina or police work.

You've taken on a mighty pretty job of piecework,

Because if there is one thing in which everybody's home-
team friends are unerring,

It is to confine their conversation to mutual acquaint-

ances and episodes as to which your visiting friends
have no idea of to what they are referring.
Most people are only vocal
When talking local.

THE BEGGAR
(After William Blake)

Beggar, beggar, burning low
In the city's trodden snow,
What immortal hand or eye
Could frame thy dread asymmetry?

In what distant deep of lies
Died the fire of thine eyes?
What the mind that planned the shame?
What the hand dare quench the flame?

And what shoulder and what art
Could rend the sinews of thy heart?
And when thy heart began to fail,
What soft excuse, what easy tale?

What the hammer? What the chain?
What the furnace dulled thy brain?
What the anvil? What the blow
Dare to forge this deadly woe?

When the business cycle ends
In flaming extra dividends,

Will He smile his work to see?
Did He who made the Ford make thee?

SHRINKING SONG

Woollen socks, woollen socks!
Full of color, full of clocks!
Plain and fancy, yellow, blue,
From the counter beam at you.
O golden fleece, O magic flocks!
O irresistible woollen socks!
O happy haberdasher's clerk
Amid that galaxy to work!
And now it festers, now it rankles
Not to have them round your ankles;
Now with your conscience do you spar;
They look expensive, and they are;
Now conscience whispers, You ought not to,
And human nature roars, You've got to!
Woollen socks, woollen socks!
First you buy them in a box.
You buy them several sizes large,
Fit for Hercules, or a barge.
You buy them thus because you think
These lovely woollen socks may shrink.
At home you don your socks with ease,
You find the heels contain your knees;
You realize with saddened heart
Their toes and yours are far apart.
You take them off and mutter Bosh,

You up and send them to the wash.
Too soon, too soon the socks return,
Too soon the horrid truth you learn;
Your woollen socks cannot be worn
Unless a midget child is born,
And either sockless you must go,
Or buy a sock for every toe.
Woollen socks, woollen socks!
Infuriating paradox!
Hosiery wonderful and terrible,
Heaven to wear, and yet unwearable.
The man enmeshed in such a quandary
Can only hie him to the laundry,
And while his socks are hung to dry,
Wear them once as they're shrinking by.

YOU CAD, WHY DON'T YOU CRINGE?

"Like most knaves he was a coward at heart . . ."
The Thirteenth Chime, *by T. C. H. Jacobs, p.*94.
"Like most knaves he was a coward at heart . . ."
Ibid, *p.* 238.

If wishes were horses every panhandler would handle
    his pan while urging a fiery steed on,
And if turnips were watches they'd make as good eating
    as turnips, which in the first place are about as ap-
    petizing as watches to feed on,
And if most knaves were cowards at heart
Everything would be as simple as Mr. T. C. H. Jacobs's
    art.
Ah, if none but the good were brave,

How well would the bad behave!

Yes, if none but the bad were poltroons

Life for the good would be all cakes and ale and ice
cream and macaroons,

And the world would be less hag-ridden,

And the air-waves less whatever-is-to-follow-Prague-rid-
den;

The future would be more wonderful,

And less blood and thunderful,

And very much less Nazi,

And very much more hotsy-totsy.

What a pity then that so many knaves haven't troubled
to study their part,

Because obviously they don't realize that they are only
cowards at heart,

And golly, what can you do with a knave

When he doesn't realize that like a coward at heart he
is supposed to behave?

Particularly when the knave seems to be a creature of
whim,

And believes that if you have something he wants it is
you who are the knave and therefore it is you who
like all knaves are a coward at heart and not him?

I think that Mr. T. C. H. Jacobs has a splendid idea, but
I also think it is up to him to make the start;

I think he should follow the arrantest knave he can find
into a dark alley or a Polish corridor at midnight
and convince him first that he is a knave and second that he is a coward at heart,

And should he happily survive,

Why he can continue until he has convinced all other
knaves alive,

And their too too solid hearts into knavish cowardice
    will melt,
And life will at last become truly heavenly and svelte.

YES AND NO

Oh would I were a politician,
Or else a person with a mission.
Heavens, how happy I could be
If only I were sure of me.

How would I strut, could I believe
That, out of all the sons of Eve,
God had granted this former youth
A binding option on His truth.

One side of the moon we've seen alone;
The other she has never shown.
What dreamless sleep, what sound digestion,
Were it the same with every question!

Sometimes with secret pride I sigh
To think how tolerant am I;
Then wonder which is really mine:
Tolerance, or a rubber spine?

FIRST PAYMENT DEFERRED

Let us look into the matter of debt
Which is something that the longer you live, why the
    deeper into it you get,

Because in the first place every creditor is their debtor's
    keeper,
And won't let you get into debt in the first place unless
    you are capable of getting in deeper,
Which is an unfortunate coincidence
Because every debtor who is capable of getting deeper
    into debt is attracted only to creditors who will en-
    courage him to get deeper into debt, which is a
    most fabulous and unfair You-were-a-creditor-in-
    Babylon-and-I-was-a-Christian-debtor Elinor Glyn-
    cidence.
Some debtors start out with debts which are little ones,
Such as board and lodging and victual ones;
Other debtors start out by never demanding that their
    bills be itemized,
Which means that they are bitten by little creditors
    upon the backs of bigger creditors and are so on ad
    infinitumized.
Veteran debtors dabble in stocks,
Or their families get adenoids or appendicitis or pox,
Any of which means that debt is what they get be-
    neather and beneather,
Either to them who told them about the stocks or to
    them who administer the chloroform and ether.
Some debts are fun while you are acquiring them,
But none are fun when you set about retiring them,
So you think you will reform, you think instead of sink-
    ing into debt you will ascend into credit,
So you live on a budget and save twenty-five per cent of
    your salary and cut corners and generally audit and
    edit,
And that is the soundest idea yet,

Because pretty soon your credit is so good that you can
    charge anything you want and settle down for eter-
    nity into peaceful and utterly irremediable debt.

MA, WHAT'S A BANKER?
or
HUSH, MY CHILD

The North wind doth blow,
And we shall have snow,
And what will the banker do then, poor thing?
Will he go to the barn
To keep himself warm,
And hide his head under his wing?
Is he on the spot, poor thing, poor thing?
Probably not, poor thing.

For when he is good,
He is not very good,
And when he is bad he is horrider,
And the chances are fair
He is taking the air
Beside a cabaña in Florida.
But the wailing investor, mean thing, mean thing,
Disturbs his siesta, poor thing.

He will plunge in the pool,
But he makes it a rule
To plunge with his kith and his kin,
And whisper about
That it's time to get out

When the widows and orphans get in.
He only got out, poor thing, poor thing,
Yet they call him a tout, poor thing.

His heart simply melts
For everyone else;
By love and compassion he's ridden;
The pay of his clerks
To reduce, how it irks!
But he couldn't go South if he didden.
I'm glad there's a drink within reach, poor thing,
As he weeps on the beach, poor thing.

May he someday find peace
In a temple in Greece,
Where the Government harbors no rancor;
May Athens and Sparta
Play host to the martyr,
And purchase a bond from the banker.
With the banker in Greece, poor thing, poor thing,
We can cling to our fleece, Hot Cha!

THE CANARY

The song of canaries
Never varies,
And when they're moulting
They're pretty revolting.

Just imagine yourself seated on a shadowy terrace,
And beside you is a girl who stirs you more strangely
    than an heiress.
It is a summer evening at its most superb,
And the moonlight reminds you that To Love is an
    active verb,
And the stars are twinkling like anything,
And a distant orchestra is playing some sentimental old
    Vienna thing,
And your hand clasps hers, which rests there without
    shrinking,
And after a silence fraught with romance you ask her
    what she is thinking,
And she starts and returns from the moon-washed dis-
    tances to the shadowy veranda,
And says, Oh I was wondering how many bamboo
    shoots a day it takes to feed a baby Giant Panda.
Or you stand with her on a hilltop and gaze on a winter
    sunset,
And everything is as starkly beautiful as a page from
    Sigrid Undset,
And your arm goes round her waist and you make an
    avowal which for masterfully marshaled emotional
    content might have been a page of Ouida's or
    Thackeray's,
And after a silence fraught with romance she says, I
    forgot to order the limes for the Daiquiris.
Or in a twilight drawing room you have just asked the
    most momentous of questions,
And after a silence fraught with romance she says I

think this little table would look better where that
little table is, but then where would that little
table go, have you any suggestions?
And that's the way they go around hitting below our
belts;
It isn't that nothing is sacred to them, it's just that
at the Sacred Moment they are always thinking of
something else.

BABY, WHAT MAKES THE SKY BLUE?

Oh, what a tangled web do parents weave
When they think that their children are naïve.
The sleighride they embark on is strenuous
When they deem their offspring ingenuous,
And particularly climb they voluntarily into the tumbril
like doomed aristocrats
When they consider themselves to be sophistocrats,
Because the moment they look on their little ones as
country cousins and themselves as suave and so-
phisticated,
Why, that is the moment they are not only going to
get their feelings hurt but also end up totally baf-
fled and mysticated,
Because you take sophisticated you, and you know that
your radio is more magical than anything out of
Andersen or the Brothers Grimm,
But you take ingenuous Junior, and it's just a radio to
him,
And you carefully explain all about Marconi and sound

waves and static and where the broadcast comes
from and how it gets here to the tot,
And he simply says Why not?
Yes, one very good reason children should be seen and
not heard
Is that to ingenuous them, an automobile or a telephone
or an electric refrigerator is no more awe-inspiring
than a flower or a bird,
Because they quickly get used to living in a world that
every day produces something that if they didn't
cultivate a calm acceptance of the impossible
would strain their belief,
So their approach to gadgets is that if they can accept
the sun and moon why they guess they can accept
the Yankee Clipper and the Super-Chief.
Sophisticated parents live agog in a world that to them
is enchanted;
Ingenuous children just naïvely take it for granted.

THE MIND OF PROFESSOR PRIMROSE

My story begins in the town of Cambridge, Mass.,
Home of the Harvard Business and Dental Schools,
And more or less the home of Harvard College.
Now, Harvard is a cultural institution,
Squandering many a dollar upon professors,
As a glance at a Harvard football team makes obvious;
Professors wise and prowling in search of wisdom,
And every mother's son of them absent-minded.
But the absentest mind belonged to Professor Primrose.

He had won a Nobel award and a Pulitzer Prize,
A Guggenheim and a leg on the Davis Cup,
But he couldn't remember to shave both sides of his
    face.
He discharged the dog and took the cook for an airing;
He frequently lit his hair and combed his cigar;
He set a trap for the baby and dandled the mice;
He wound up his key and opened the door with his
    watch;
He tipped his students and flunked the traffic police-
    man;
He fed the mosquitoes crumbs and slapped at the
    robins;
He always said his prayers when he entered the theater,
And left the church for a smoke between the acts;
He mixed the exterminator man a cocktail
And told his guests to go way, he had no bugs;
He rode the streets on a bicycle built for two,
And he never discovered he wasn't teaching at Yale.
At last one summer he kissed his crimson flannels
And packed his wife in camphor, and she complained.
She had always hated camphor, and she complained.
"My dear," she ordered, "these contretemps must cease;
You must bring this absent mind a little bit nearer;
You must tidy up that disorderly cerebellum;
You must write today and enroll in the Pelman Insti-
    tute."
He embraced his pen and he took his wife in hand,
He wrinkled a stamp and thoughtfully licked his brow,
He wrote the letter and mailed it, and what do you
    know?
In a couple of days he disappeared from Cambridge.

"For heaven's sake, my husband has disappeared,"
Said Mrs. Primrose. "Now isn't that just like him?"
And she cut the meat and grocery orders in half,
And moved the chairs in the living room around,
And settled down to a little solid comfort.
She had a marvelous time for seven years,
At the end of which she took a train to Chicago.
She liked to go to Chicago once in a while
Because of a sister-in-law who lived in Cambridge.
Her eye was caught at Schenectady by the porter;
She noticed that he was brushing off a dime,
And trying to put the passenger in his pocket.
"Porter," she said, "aren't you Professor Primrose?
Aren't you my husband, the missing Professor Prim-
    rose?
And what did you learn at the Pelman Institute?"
"Mah Lawd, Maria," the porter said, "mah Lawd!
Did you say Pelman? Ah wrote to de Pullman folks!"

REFLECTION ON CAUTION

Affection is a noble quality;
It leads to generosity and jollity.
But it also leads to breach of promise
If you go around lavishing it on red-hot momise.

MIDSUMMER'S DAYMARE

Mumbo jumbo, what have we here?
Why we have the longest day in the year.

· 87 ·

This is the rarest day of June,
And it's weeks and weeks from dawn to noon.
This is the calendar's blazing highlight,
It's months and months from noon to twilight.
Lucky are they who retain their friends
Through the day that seldom if ever ends.
Take a modest date, like December twenty,
And still the telephone jangles plenty,
Still you encounter bores enough,
Obligations and chores enough,
Visitors to avoid enough
Like something out of Freud enough,
Creditors, editors, tears and combats,
Newsreel beauties embracing wombats,
Feeble coffee and vanishing waiters,
Newsreel girls riding alligators,
Traffic and taxes and dues and duties
And candidates kissing newsreel beauties.
Oh, man has need of all his strength
To survive a day of medium length;
What wonder, then, that man grows bitter
On a day that sits like a flagpole-sitter?
Mumbo jumbo, noon infernal,
This, my dear, is the day eternal.
You toil for a dollar or two per diem,
You mope and hope for the blessed P.M.,
You look at the clock, you're ready for mayhem;
Is it P.M. yet? No, it's still the A.M.!
On farm and field, in office and park,
This is the day that won't get dark.
Dusk is an exile, night has fled,
Never again shall we get to bed,

The sun has swallowed the moon and stars,
Midnight lies with the buried Czars.
This is the guerdon of prayer and fasting:
Glorious day, day everlasting!

I NEVER EVEN SUGGESTED IT

I know lots of men who are in love and lots of men
who are married and lots of men who are both,
And to fall out with their loved ones is what all of them
are most loth.
They are conciliatory at every opportunity,
Because all they want is serenity and a certain amount
of impunity.
Yes, many the swain who has finally admitted that the
earth is flat
Simply to sidestep a spat,
Many the masculine Positively or Absolutely which has
been diluted to an If
Simply to avert a tiff,
Many the two-fisted executive whose domestic conver-
sation is limited to a tactfully interpolated Yes,
And then he is amazed to find that he is being raked
backwards over a bed of coals nevertheless.
These misguided fellows are under the impression that
it takes two to make a quarrel, that you can side-
step a crisis by nonaggression and nonresistance,
Instead of removing yourself to a discreet distance.
Passivity can be a provoking modus operandi;
Consider the Empire and Gandhi.

Silence is golden, but sometimes invisibility is golder.

Because loved ones may not be able to make bricks
without straw but often they don't need any straw
to manufacture a bone to pick or blood in their eye
or a chip for their soft white shoulder.

It is my duty, gentlemen, to inform you that women
are dictators all, and I recommend to you this
moral:

In real life it takes only one to make a quarrel.

MY DEAR, HOW EVER DID YOU THINK UP THIS DELICIOUS SALAD?

This is a very sad ballad,

Because it's about the way too many people make a
salad.

Generally they start with bananas,

And they might just as well use gila monsters or
iguanas.

Pineapples are another popular ingredient,

Although there is one school that holds preserved pears
or peaches more expedient,

And you occasionally meet your fate

In the form of a prune or a date.

Rarely you may chance to discover a soggy piece of
tomato looking very forlorn and Cinderella-ry,

But for the most part you are confronted by apples and
celery,

And it's not a bit of use at this point to turn pale or
break out in a cold perspiration,

Because all this is only the foundation,

Because if you think the foundation sounds unenticing,
Just wait until we get to the dressing, or rather, the
    icing.
There are various methods of covering up the body,
    and to some, marshmallows are the pall supreme,
And others prefer whipped cream,
And then they deck the grave with ground-up peanuts
    and maraschinos
And you get the effect of a funeral like Valentino's,
And about the only thing that in this kind of salad is
    never seen
Is any kind of green,
And oil and vinegar and salt and pepper are at a mini-
    mum,
But there is a maximum of sugar and syrup and ginger
    and nutmeg and cinnamum,
And my thoughts about this kind of salad are just as
    unutterable
As parsnips are unbutterable,
And indeed I am surprised that the perpetrators haven't
    got around to putting buttered parsnips in these
    salmagundis,
And the salad course nowadays seems to be a month of
    sundaes.

WHAT'S THE USE?

Sure, deck your lower limbs in pants;
Yours are the limbs, my sweeting.
You look divine as you advance —
Have you seen yourself retreating?

Foreigners are people somewhere else,
Natives are people at home;
If the place you're at is your habitat,
You're a foreigner, say in Rome.
But the scales of Justice balance true,
And tit only leads to tat,
So the man who's at home when he stays in Rome
Is abroad when he's where you're at.

When we leave the limits of the land in which
Our birth certificates sat us,
It does not mean just a change of scene,
But also a change of status.
The Frenchman with his fetching beard,
The Scot with his kilt and sporran,
One moment he may a native be,
And the next may find him foreign.

There's many a difference quickly found
Between the different races,
But the only essential differential
Is living in different places.
Yet such is the pride of prideful man,
From Austrians to Australians,
That wherever he is, he regards as his,
And the natives there, as aliens.

Oh, I'll be friends if you'll be friends,
The foreigner tells the native,
And we'll work together for our common ends
Like a preposition and a dative.

If our common ends seem mostly mine,
Why not, you ignorant foreigner?
And the native replies contrariwise;
And hence, my dears, the coroner.

So mind your manners when a native, please,
And doubly when you're not,
And Vickers and Krupp will soon fold up,
And Sopwith pawn his yacht.
One simple thought, if you have it pat,
Will eliminate the coroner:
You may be a native in your habitat,
But to foreigners you're just a foreigner.

OH, STOP BEING THANKFUL ALL OVER
THE PLACE

Too many people go around clapping till their palms
    are covered with calluses
At comments which sound simply splendid but turn
    out to be compounded of fusel oil and burnt sugar
    and very weak wood alcohol when subjected to
    analluses.
In this glittering collection of paste diamonds one in
    particular ranks very high,
And that is the often-quoted remark of the prominent
    and respectable dignitary who on seeing a con-
    demned man on his way to the scaffold crashed
    into a thousand anthologies by remarking, There
    but for the grace of God go I.
Here is a deplorable illustration

Of sloppy ratiocination;

Here is a notable feat

Of one-way thinking on a two-way street.

It must certainly have been the speaker's lucky day,

Or otherwise he would have been run over by his speech turning around and coming back the other way,

Because did he stop to work out his premise to its logical conclusion? Ah no,

He just got it off and let it go,

And now whenever people are with people they want to impress with their combined greatheartedness and book-learning they cry

Oh look at that condemned man on his way to the scaffold, there but for the grace of God go I.

Which is so far so good, but they neglect to continue with the heretofore unspoken balance of the theme, which is equally true,

That there but for the grace of God goes Jimmie Durante or the Prince of Wales or Aimee Semple McPherson or Dr. Wellington Koo,

Or Moses or Napoleon or Cleopatra or King Midas,

Or a man named Harris who is just getting over an attack of tonsilidas,

And to take one more step just to keep the record straight, I insist that, but for this divine grace which they appropriate so glibly to their own eloquent purposes because they want to appear both scholarly and well-intentioned,

But for this divine grace, I say, they themselves might be not only the malefactor who serves as a springboard for their dive into pious platitudes, but John

D. Rockefeller or Senator Hiram Johnson or Greta
Garbo or anybody at all possibly better, possibly
worse off than they are, including Dr. Wellington
Koo and the others I have previously mentioned.
So away with you, all you parrot-like repeaters of high-
sounding phrases that you never stop to consider
what they actually mean,
I wouldn't allow you to stay in any college of which I
was the Dean.
I can never listen to you without thinking Oh my,
There but for the grace of God speak I.

ARTHUR

There was an old man of Calcutta,
Who coated his tonsils with butta,
Thus converting his snore
From a thunderous roar
To a soft, oleaginous mutta.

EVERYBODY EATS TOO MUCH ANYHOW

You gulp your breakfast and glance at the clock,
Through eleventh-hour packing you gallop amok,
You bundle your bags in the back of the car,
You enter, she enters, and there you are.
You clutch the wheel, she clutches the maps,
And longs for a couple of extra laps.
It's au revoir to your modest abode,

You're gypsies, away on the open road;
Into the highway you burst like a comet or
Heat waves climbing a Kansas thermometer.
The conversation is sweet as clover,
With breakfast practically hardly over.
"Darling, light me a cigarette?"
"At once and with all my heart, my pet;
And by the way, we are off the track;
We should have turned left a half-mile back."
You swing around with a cheery smile,
Thus far, a mile is only a mile.
The road is romance, so let it wind,
With breakfast an hour or so behind.
Under the tires the pebbles crunch,
And through the dust creep thoughts of lunch.
The speedometer sits on a steady fifty
And more and more does lunch seem nifty.
Your eyes to the road ahead are glued,
She glances about in search of food.
She sees a place. She would like to try it.
She says so. Well, you're already by it.
Ignoring the road, you spot an eatery;
The look of it makes her interior teetery.
She sees a beauty. You're past it again.
Her eyebrows look like ten past ten;
She's simmering now, and so are you,
And your brows register ten to two.
She snubs the excuse as you begin it:
That there'll be another one any minute,
She says there won't. It must be a plot;
She's absolutely correct. There's not.
You finally find one. You stop and alight.

You're both too annoyed to eat a bite.
Oh, this is the gist of my gypsy song:
Next time carry your lunch along.

THE RHINOCEROS

The rhino is a homely beast,
For human eyes he's not a feast.
Farewell, farewell, you old rhinoceros,
I'll stare at something less prepoceros.

SONG TO BE SUNG BY THE FATHER
OF INFANT FEMALE CHILDREN

My heart leaps up when I behold
A rainbow in the sky;
Contrariwise, my blood runs cold
When little boys go by.
For little boys as little boys,
No special hate I carry,
But now and then they grow to men,
And when they do, they marry.
No matter how they tarry,
Eventually they marry.
And, swine among the pearls,
They marry little girls.

Oh, somewhere, somewhere, an infant plays,
With parents who feed and clothe him.

Their lips are sticky with pride and praise,
But I have begun to loathe him.
Yes, I loathe with a loathing shameless
This child who to me is nameless.
This bachelor child in his carriage
Gives never a thought to marriage,
But a person can hardly say knife
Before he will hunt him a wife.

I never see an infant (male),
A-sleeping in the sun,
Without I turn a trifle pale
And think, is he the one?
Oh, first he'll want to crop his curls,
And then he'll want a pony,
And then he'll think of pretty girls
And holy matrimony.
He'll put away his pony,
And sigh for matrimony.
A cat without a mouse
Is he without a spouse.

Oh, somewhere he bubbles bubbles of milk,
And quietly sucks his thumbs.
His cheeks are roses painted on silk,
And his teeth are tucked in his gums.
But alas, the teeth will begin to grow,
And the bubbles will cease to bubble;
Given a score of years or so,
The roses will turn to stubble.
He'll sell a bond, or he'll write a book,
And his eyes will get that acquisitive look,

And raging and ravenous for the kill,
He'll boldly ask for the hand of Jill.
This infant whose middle
Is diapered still
Will want to marry
My daughter Jill.

Oh sweet be his slumber and moist his middle!
My dreams, I fear, are infanticiddle.
A fig for embryo Lohengrins!
I'll open all of his safety pins,
I'll pepper his powder, and salt his bottle,
And give him readings from Aristotle.
Sand for his spinach I'll gladly bring,
And Tabasco sauce for his teething ring,
And an elegant, elegant alligator
To play with in his perambulator.
Then perhaps he'll struggle through fire and water
To marry somebody else's daughter.

ONE FROM ONE LEAVES TWO

Higgledy piggledy, my black hen,
She lays eggs for gentlemen.
Gentlemen come every day
To count what my black hen doth lay.
If perchance she lays too many,
They fine my hen a pretty penny;
If perchance she fails to lay,
The gentlemen a bonus pay.

Mumbledy pumbledy, my red cow,
She's co-operating now.
At first she didn't understand
That milk production must be planned;
She didn't understand at first
She either had to plan or burst,
But now the Government reports
She's giving pints instead of quarts.

Fiddle de dee, my next-door neighbors,
They are giggling at their labors.
First they plant the tiny seed,
Then they water, then they weed,
Then they hoe and prune and lop,
Then they raise a record crop,
Then they laugh their sides asunder,
And plow the whole kaboodle under.

Abracadabra, thus we learn
The more you create, the less you earn.
The less you earn, the more you're given,
The less you lead, the more you're driven,
The more destroyed, the more they feed,
The more you pay, the more they need,
The more you earn, the less you keep,
And now I lay me down to sleep.

I pray the Lord my soul to take
If some Soul Commission hasn't got it before I wake.

GENEALOGICAL REFLECTION

No McTavish
Was ever lavish.

THERE'S A HOST BORN EVERY MINUTE

Week ends are things that you get into the habit of
    asking people to stay with you during,
Which is a habit that there is no way of curing.
When you first decide you want somebody to come and
    spend a week end with you you start out by ask-
    ing people you'd be very glad to have in your
    home,
But they are always having a baby or tied up at the
    office working on codes or on the point of depar-
    ture for Rio de Janeiro or Nome,
So then you ask somebody that while you aren't crazy
    about them still you don't really mind them,
And it turns out that they aren't in the telephone book
    or have just moved or something and there is no
    way to find them.
You are by now so annoyed
That you go right ahead and ask a lot of people that
    you've been spending the previous part of your life
    trying to avoid,
And they arrive and you give up your bathroom to
    them and go in and bathe with your baby or tot,
And all the thanks you get is a remark that the hot
    water isn't very hot,
And may I be guillotined by a guillotiner or garroted by
    a garroter or arched by an archer

If that isn't about the jolliest thing that happens from
    their arrival to their departure.
The week end is just the week's caboose,
But it's not nearly of so much use,
And some prophet who dreams dreams and sees visions
Ought to warn everybody that with weeks as well as
    with railroad trains we ought all to look out for
    rear-end collisions.

TELL IT TO THE ESKIMOS
or
TELL IT TO THE ESQUIMAUX

Jonathan Jukes is full of health,
And he doesn't care who knows it.
Others may exercise by stealth,
But he with a cry of Prosit!
Others put up with coated tongues,
And shoulders narrow and droopy;
Jonathan overinflates his lungs
With a thundering shout of Whoopee!
Jonathan's noise is healthy noise,
Jonathan's joys are healthy joys,
Jonathan shuns the primrose path,
And starts the day with an icy bath.

I might forgive the super-physique
Contained in the Jukes apparel;
The apple glowing in either cheek;
The chest like an oyster barrel;

The muscles that flow like a mountain stream,
The result of applied eugenics;
The rigorous diet, the stern régime
Of arduous calisthenics;
I can pardon most of the healthy joys,
I can pardon most of the healthy noise,
But Heaven itself no pardon hath
For the man who boasts of an icy bath.

If the Missing Links were vigorous chaps
And their manly deeds were myriad,
Must civilization then relapse
Back to the glacial period?
Humanity learns at a fearful price;
Must the lessons all be lost?
Does the locomotive feed on ice?
Is the liner propelled by frost?

One constant truth mankind has found
Through fire and flood and slaughter:
The thing that makes the wheels go round
Is plenty of good hot water.
And therefore, therefore, Jonathan Jukes,
You deserve the harshest of harsh rebukes;
You and your frigid daily bath
Are blocking civilization's path.
You think of yourself as Spartan and spunky?
So, Jonathan, is the old brass monkey.

One thing that literature would be greatly the better
for
Would be a more restricted employment by authors
of simile and metaphor.
Authors of all races, be they Greeks, Romans, Teutons
or Celts,
Can't seem just to say that anything is the thing it is
but have to go out of their way to say that it is
like something else.
What does it mean when we are told
That the Assyrian came down like a wolf on the fold?
In the first place, George Gordon Byron had had
enough experience
To know that it probably wasn't just one Assyrian, it
was a lot of Assyrians.
However, as too many arguments are apt to induce apo-
plexy and thus hinder longevity,
We'll let it pass as one Assyrian for the sake of brevity.
Now then, this particular Assyrian, the one whose cohorts were gleaming in purple and gold,
Just what does the poet mean when he says he came
down like a wolf on the fold?
In heaven and earth more than is dreamed of in our
philosophy there are a great many things,
But I don't imagine that among them there is a wolf
with purple and gold cohorts or purple and gold
anythings.
No, no, Lord Byron, before I'll believe that this Assyrian was actually like a wolf I must have some
kind of proof;

Did he run on all fours and did he have a hairy tail and
a big red mouth and big white teeth and did he
say Woof woof woof?

Frankly I think it very unlikely, and all you were entitled to say, at the very most,

Was that the Assyrian cohorts came down like a lot
of Assyrian cohorts about to destroy the Hebrew
host.

But that wasn't fancy enough for Lord Byron, oh dear
me no, he had to invent a lot of figures of speech
and then interpolate them,

With the result that whenever you mention Old Testa-
ment soldiers to people they say Oh yes, they're
the ones that a lot of wolves dressed up in gold
and purple ate them.

That's the kind of thing that's being done all the time
by poets, from Homer to Tennyson;

They're always comparing ladies to lilies and veal to
venison,

And they always say things like that the snow is a white
blanket after a winter storm.

Oh it is, is it, all right then, you sleep under a six-inch
blanket of snow and I'll sleep under a half-inch
blanket of unpoetical blanket material and we'll
see which one keeps warm,

And after that maybe you'll begin to comprehend
dimly

What I mean by too much metaphor and simile.

THE LAMB

Little gamboling lamb,
Do you know where you am?
In a patch of mint.
I'll give you a hint:
Scram,
Lamb!

THE STRANGE CASE OF MR. GOODBODY
or
A TEAM THAT WON'T BE BEATEN,
CAN'T BE BEATEN

Once upon a time there was a man named Mr. Goodbody.

⁕

He was the Dean of Notary Publics.

⁕

He often told his intimates, My commission expires
November 1, 1934.

⁕

He simply adored lobster.

⁕

Nevertheless, he eschewed the tasty crustacean.

⁕

My career comes first, said Mr. Goodbody.

⁕

I like lobster, he said, but lobster doesn't like me.

⁕

His hearers set this down to false modesty.

⁕

It's only Mr. Goodbody's false modesty, they said.

∾

They said that all the world and his wife like Mr. Goodbody.

∾

Mr. Goodbody only smiled.

∾

Mr. Goodbody was indeed Dean of Notary Publics.

∾

One day Mr. Goodbody consulted a calendar and found it was October 31, 1934.

∾

It is Commission-Expiration Eve, said Mr. Goodbody.

∾

Tonight I shall eat, drink and be merry, for tomorrow I am Dean-Emeritus of Notary Publics.

∾

Mr. Goodbody's man, Roosevelt, suggested a cold bird and a bottle.

∾

May I suggest a cold bird and a bottle sir? said Roosevelt.

∾

Mr. Goodbody asked Roosevelt if he was any relation to the Roosevelt.

∾

All Roosevelts are the Roosevelt, said Roosevelt.

∾

Well anyhow I don't want a cold bird and a bottle, said Mr. Goodbody.

∾

Perhaps a deviled kidney? said Roosevelt. Or a grilled
bone?

∾

No, said Mr. Goodbody.

∾

Roosevelt said, Then what do you want, for God's sake?

∾

A great big lobster, said Mr. Goodbody.

∾

It was two hours past dinnertime when Mr. Goodbody
walked into the kitchen.

∾

He said that it was two hours past dinnertime, and where
was dinner?

∾

Roosevelt said that he begged his pardon, sir, but that
the lobster wouldn't boil.

∾

The first hour it had spent in a steady Australian crawl,
he said.

∾

The next hour was given over to practising a fancy
backstroke.

∾

At the moment, he said, it was treading water.

∾

He said that it took to boiling water like a secret marriage to the front page.

∾

Serve it at once, said Mr. Goodbody.

∾

Roosevelt said that he begged his pardon, sir, but the lobster wasn't cooked.

⁓

Mr. Goodbody asked was he or was he not Dean-Emeritus of Notary Publics?

⁓

He said he rather thought he was and any lobster that had been boiling for two hours and a half was boiled.

⁓

Roosevelt said that he was sorry, sir, but he could see for himself that the lobster was still green.

⁓

Mr. Goodbody said that it was red because it had been boiling for two hours and a half and had to be red, and it was to be served at once.

⁓

Furthermore he said that he wanted Roosevelt to ask him, Mr. Goodbody, what he, Mr. Goodbody, would say if he, Roosevelt, found him, Mr. Goodbody, eating with his bare hands and said that such a spectacle would shock the author of the Gunpowder Plot.

⁓

Roosevelt asked him.

⁓

I would say, Fingers were made before Fawkes, said Mr. Goodbody.

⁓

Roosevelt gladly served the lobster.

⁓

What a beautiful boiled lobster! said Mr. Goodbody.

The long swim had given the lobster quite an appetite.

It seized one of Mr. Goodbody's fingers in its claws.

Perfectly delicious, said Mr. Goodbody.

Cooked to a turn, he said.

A veritable dish for a Dean-Emeritus of Notary Publics, he said.

Mr. Goodbody and the lobster fell to with a will.

Some time later Mr. Goodbody had deserted the table for the dimly-lit interior of the lobster.

He was smiling a satisfied smile.

That was the best lobster I ever ate, said Mr. Goodbody.

THE WAPITI

There goes the Wapiti,
Hippety-hoppity!

THE CASE OF IDENTITY

Some people achieve temporary fame
Because they never forget the face but never remember
    the name,
And others set a dizzy pace
By never missing a name but never recognizing a face,
And still others are sharpshooters for both names and
    faces and can at a glance fasten them to their
    proprietors in their proper positions,
And you want to look out for people with this charm-
    ing social gift because they are either salesmen or
    politicians,
And finally there is a fourth unfortunate class of people
    who are constantly so embarrassed that they wish
    they could be swallowed up by a dozen Atlantics
    or Pacifics,
Because to their astigmatic eyes and wandering minds,
    faces are but a bouillabaisse of features, and names
    but an omelet of hieroglyphics,
And if you too, dear reader, belong to this unhappy
    group,
I fear your life contains more woe-is-me than boop-
    boop-a-doop.
People come up to you and say You don't remember
    me, do you, and of course you say you do, and
    of course you don't,
And the first two or three times it happens you think
    maybe they will eventually identify themselves but
    finally you get to know that they consistently
    won't,

And then when you walk along the street you are never
off the horns of a dilemma,
Because you are always seeing somebody that you think
you know but you can't quite rememma,
And if you don't speak to them they invariably turn
out to have been somebody you like or somebody
you like's wife,
And they get very angry and tell everybody you aren't
speaking to your old friends any more and they
are off you for life,
And if you do speak to them, of the nearest policeman
you are in danger
Because they invariably turn out to be a suspicious
feminine stranger.
Then if you ever do happen to get a name by heart
It generally belongs to some single lady who immediately gets married or some married lady who immediately resumes her single name and you have
to go back and make a fresh start.
And another thing you have to get used to
Is introducing people to people when you can't remember either the name of the people who are to be
introduced or the people they are supposed to be
introduced to,
And I wish all the people who are good at names or
faces or both would retire to St. Helena or Elba
or Taos,
And leave the rest of us to live quietly in cozy anony-
mous chaos.

READ THIS VIBRANT EXPOSÉ

Now curfew tolls in the old church steeple,
Bidding good night to sensible people;
Now thousands and thousands of people sensible
Think staying up later is reprehensible;
Now wives relentlessly bridge games terminate,
As thoughts of the morrow begin to germinate;
Now gangsters with pistols full of notches
Yawn discreetly and glance at their watches;
Now owls desist from to-wit-to-wooing,
And ne'er-do-wells from their ne'er-well-doing;
Now husband and wife and spouse and spouse
Unleash their cat and lock up their house;
Now celibates, of whom there are lots,
Wearily seek their lonely cots;
Now, in a word, the day is ended,
And a little sleep would be simply splendid.
But sleep is perverse as human nature,
Sleep is perverse as a legislature,
And holds that people who wish to sleep
Are people from whom away to keep.
Sleep, I am more than sorry to say,
Is deliberately half a world away.

The curfew that tolls in yonder steeple
Is unheard by a hemisphere of people.
Across the world, the alarm clock's reveille
Wakes foreigners drowsy and dishevelly;
Across the world the sun is aloft,
And people must rise from their mattresses soft,
And polish their teeth and shine their faces

And go to work in various places.
Now opens wide their portal of day,
And sleep, you might think, would go away,
Sleep would abandon that hemisphere
And distribute its favors over here.
But sleep is perverse as human nature,
Sleep is perverse as a legislature,
Sleep is as forward as hives or goiters,
And where it is least desired, it loiters.
Sleep is as shy as a maiden sprite,
And where it is most desired, takes flight.
So people who go to bed to sleep
Must count French premiers or sheep,
And people who ought to arise from bed
Yawn and go back to sleep instead.

And you can pile all the poems in the world in a heap,
And this is the first to tell the truth about sleep.

REFLECTION ON A COMMON MISAPPREHENSION

So many forthright ladies are overjoyed
To think themselves hard-boiled when as a matter of
    fact they are only Freud.

Husbands are things that wives have to get used to
    putting up with,
And with whom they breakfast with and sup with.
They interfere with the discipline of nurseries,
And forget anniversaries,
And when they have been particularly remiss
They think they can cure everything with a great big
    kiss.
They are annoying when they stay home
And even more annoying when they roam,
And when you tell them about something they have
    done they just look unbearably patient and smile
    a superior smile,
And think, Oh she'll get over it after a while,
And they always drink cocktails faster than they can
    assimilate them,
And if you look in their direction they act as if they
    were martyrs and you were trying to sacrifice, or
    immolate them.
And when it's a question of walking five miles to play
    golf they are very energetic but if it's doing any-
    thing useful around the house they are very le-
    thargic,
And then they tell you that women are unreasonable
    and don't know anything about logic,
And they never want to get up or go to bed at the same
    time as you do,
And when you perform some simple common or gar-
    den rite like putting cold cream on your face or

applying a touch of lipstick they seem to think
you are up to some kind of black magic like a
priestess of Voodoo,

And if you serve meat balls for dinner they look put-
upon and say Can't we ever have a sirloin or a
porterhouse,

So you get them what they want and then when the
bills come in they act as if you were trying to drive
them to the slorterhouse,

And they are brave and calm and cool and collected
about the ailments of the person they have promised to honor and cherish,

But the minute they get a sniffle or a stomach-ache of
their own, why you'd think they were about to
perish,

And when you are alone with them they ignore all the
minor courtesies and as for airs and graces, they
utterly lack them,

But when there are a lot of people around they hand
you so many chairs and ash trays and sandwiches
and butter you with such bowings and scrapings
that you want to smack them.

Husbands are indeed an irritating form of life,

And yet through some quirk of Providence most of
them are really very deeply ensconced in the affection of their wife.

TURNS IN A WORM'S LANE

I've never bet on a so-called horse
That the horse didn't lose a leg.

I've never putted on a golfing course
But the ball behaved like an egg.
I've never possessed three royal kings
But somebody held three aces;
In short, I'm a lad whose presence brings
The joy to bankers' faces.

And everybody says, "What a splendid loser!"
Everybody says, "What a thoroughgoing sport!"
And I smile my smile like an amiable Duse,
I leer like a lawyer in the presence of a tort.
And I crack my lips,
And I grin my grin,
While someone else
Rakes my money in.
Yes, I smile a smile like the Mona Lisa,
Though my spirits droop like the Tower of Pisa.
Yes, I chortle like a military march by Sousa
And everybody says, "What a splendid loser!"

I'll buy a tome, an expensive tome,
On the gentle craft of diddling,
And I'll wrap it up and I'll take it home,
And read till I'm fair to middling.
I'll stealthily study the ebony arts
Of men like the great Houdini,
Till both in foreign and local parts
I'm known as a darned old meany.

And everyone will say, "What a nasty winner!"
And everyone will say, "What a dreadful sport!"
And they'll all stop inviting me to come to dinner,
For I used to be a dimple and I want to be a wart.

But I won't care,
And I'll win with a scowl,
Foul means or fair,
But preferably foul.

I'll jeer my victims every time I vanquish,
And if I lose I shall scream with anguish.
And people will say, "What a dreadful sport!"
And I'll say, "Phooie!" or something of the sort.

KINDLY UNHITCH THAT STAR, BUDDY

I hardly suppose I know anybody who wouldn't rather
    be a success than a failure,
Just as I suppose every piece of crabgrass in the garden
    would much rather be an azalea,
And in celestial circles all the run-of-the-mill angels
    would rather be archangels or at least cherubim
    and seraphim,
And in the legal world all the little process-servers hope
    to grow up into great big bailiffim and sheriffim.
Indeed, everybody wants to be a wow,
But not everybody knows exactly how.
Some people think they will eventually wear diamonds
    instead of rhinestones
Only by everlastingly keeping their noses to their
    ghrinestones,
And other people think they will be able to put in
    more time at Palm Beach and the Ritz
By not paying too much attention to attendance at the
    office but rather in being brilliant by starts and fits.

Some people after a full day's work sit up all night
   getting a college education by correspondence,
While others seem to think they'll get just as far by
   devoting their evenings to the study of the difference in temperament between brunettance and
   blondance.
Some stake their all on luck,
And others put their faith in their ability to pass the
   buck.
In short, the world is filled with people trying to
   achieve success,
And half of them think they'll get it by saying No and
   half of them by saying Yes,
And if all the ones who say No said Yes, and vice versa,
   such is the fate of humanity that ninety-nine per
   cent of them still wouldn't be any better off than
   they were before,
Which perhaps is just as well because if everybody was
   a success nobody could be contemptuous of anybody else and everybody would start in all over
   again trying to be a bigger success than everybody
   else so they would have somebody to be contemptuous of and so on forevermore,
Because when people start hitching their wagons to a
   star,
That's the way they are.

LITERARY REFLECTION

Philo Vance
Needs a kick in the pance.

· 119 ·

THE STRANGE CASE OF THE BAFFLED
HERMIT

Once upon a time there was a man named Mr. Oliphant.

☙

He was a hermit.

☙

Wags used to call him Mr. Elephant.

☙

That was one reason he became a hermit.

☙

The other reason was more practical.

☙

Hermits are coming back strong, said Mr. Oliphant.

☙

Conditions have never been so favorable, he said.

☙

Personally, said Mr. Oliphant, I am going to get in on the ground floor.

☙

He got in on the ground floor of the new two-hundred-story Prosperity Bank Building and didn't see anybody for three years.

☙

At first he had a little trouble with the echo.

☙

My name is Oliphant, said Mr. Oliphant.

☙

Mr. Elephant, said the echo.

☙

No, Oliphant, said Mr. Oliphant.

☙

No, Elephant, said the echo.

~

Elephant, said Mr. Oliphant.

~

Oliphant, said the echo.

~

That's more like it, said Mr. Oliphant.

~

At the end of the third year Mr. Oliphant said he certainly did like being a hermit.

~

He said his one regret was that he hadn't become a hermit sooner.

~

Anybody that wasn't a hermit didn't know anything, he said.

~

He said, Why, he hadn't heard a smoking-room story in three years.

~

Mr. Oliphant then leapt from his cell with a hell of a yell.

~

He asked a policeman to direct him to the nearest smoking-room.

~

In the smoking-room he met a Mr. Buell, a Mr. Duell, and a Mr. Newell.

~

Now for a spicy jest, thought Mr. Oliphant, his eyes gleaming through his matted locks.

~

He settled back in his chair to listen, veritably agog. Mr. Buell was telling Mr. Duell about his approach on the eighteenth at Bonnie Brassie last Sunday.

∽

Mr. Duell was telling Mr. Newell that his oldest loved spinach, but it was a funny thing, his youngest wouldn't look at it.

∽

Mr. Newell was telling Mr. Buell that his bookkeeper had just about run out of red ink.

∽

Mr. Oliphant said he hoped these gentlemen would pardon the interruption, but he was a hermit and hadn't heard a smoking-room story in three years.

∽

Mr. Buell, Mr. Duell, and Mr. Newell blushed and apologized for the vulgarity of their conversation.

∽

Mr. Oliphant left.

∽

He visited successively a barroom, a locker room, and the smoking compartment of a Pullman car.

∽

O tempora, O mores, O God, O Montreal! said Mr. Oliphant.

∽

The sturdy masculine humor of our forefathers has degenerated, said Mr. Oliphant, into business, babies, and golf.

∽

He decided to be a hermit again, but he had to stop
    by the house a minute to get a clean handkerchief.

∽

He walked quietly into the middle of a large bridge
    party given by his wife.

∽

Mr. Oliphant heard one remark and his ears grew red.

∽

He heard a second remark and his cheeks burned.

∽

In five minutes Mr. Oliphant was glowing like a hairy
    stop-light.

∽

He tiptoed back to his hermitage without the clean
    handkerchief.

∽

My name is Mr. Oliphant, he said.

∽

I don't get the name, said the echo.

∽

But the face is familiar.

MAY I DRIVE YOU HOME,
MRS. MURGATROYD?

Here's a statement that anybody who feels so inclined
    is welcome to make a hearty mental meal of:
People who possess operator's licenses ought never to
    ride in a car that anybody else is at the wheel of.
It seems to be their point of view

· 123 ·

That you are some kind of fanatic bent on murdering
      or mutilating them even in the face of the cer-
      tainty that in so doing you must murder or muti-
      late yourself too.
They are always jumping and wincing and jamming
      their feet down on an imaginary brake,
Or making noises as if they had just discovered that
      their bed was inhabited by a snake,
Or else they start a casual conversation that begins with
      remarks about the weather and other banalities,
And leads up to a pointed comment on the horrifying
      number of annual automobile fatalities.
They tell you not only about cars that actually are
      coming but also cars that might be coming, and
      they do it so kindly and gently
That it's obvious they consider you deaf and blind as
      well as rather deficient mently.
And when at last you somehow manage to get to where
      you've been going to they say thank you in a
      voice full of plaster of Paris and bitter aloes,
And get down out of the car as if they were getting
      down off the gallows,
And they walk away with the Is-it-really-over expression
      of a lot of rescued survivors
And you go off and make a lot of remarks to yourself
      about back-seat drivers,
And you vow that come what may you yourself will
      never join their ranks, no indeed,
And then the next day somebody gives you a lift and
      you find yourself bathed with cold moisture the
      moment they shift the gears into third speed.
The truth of the matter, mesdames and sirs,

Is that we are all born chauffeurs;
Or, to put it another way before retiring to curl up with
    a bad book on the sofa,
Everybody in the car can drive better than the chauffeur.

ONE THIRD OF A CALENDAR

In January everything freezes.
We have two children. Both are she'ses.
This is our January rule:
One girl in bed, and one in school.

In February the blizzard whirls.
We own a pair of little girls.
Blessings upon of each the head —
The one in school and the one in bed.

March is the month of cringe and bluster.
Each of our children has a sister.
They cling together like Hansel and Gretel,
With their noses glued to the benzoin kettle.

April is made of impetuous waters
And doctors looking down throats of daughters.
If we had a son too, and a Samoyed,
We'd have a dog,
And a boy,
And two girls
In bed.

The trouble with games of chance is that they don't do
    much to stimulate your pulse
Unless you risk some money on the results,
And the trouble with playing for money is not that it
    is a sin,
But that you have got either to lose or win,
And the trouble with losing is not only that you need
    the money, which is an important point, very true,
But also that you never lose it except to somebody who
    is very much richer than you,
And the trouble with winning, if you can bring your-
    self to imagine any trouble with winning, is that
    except in the most glamorous fiction
You never win except from somebody to whom you
    know that the money that they pay over to you
    is all that stands between them and eviction.
Another thing about games of chance
Is a thing at which I look askance,
And that is that no matter how far at any time you may
    be ahead,
You are always well behind when it is time for bed,
While on the other hand if you start out by losing as
    steadily and heavily as if you were afflicted with
    Tutankhamen's curse
You finish up even worse,
So you can take it as understood
That your luck changes only if it's good.
And this, my friends, is a brief history of the major
    troubles with gambling but I feel that no improv-
    ing lesson from it will be learned

As long as there is nothing so delightful in the world
as money you haven't earned.

OBVIOUS REFLECTION

Dentists' anterooms
Give me tanterooms.

SUPPOSE I DARKEN YOUR DOOR

It seems to me that if you must be sociable it is better
to go and see people than to have people come and
see you,
Because then you can leave when you are through.
Yes, the moment you begin to nod
You can look at your watch and exclaim Goodness gracious, it is ten o'clock already, I had no idea it
was so late, how very odd!
And you politely explain that you have to get up early
in the morning to keep an important engagement
with a man from Alaska or Siam,
And you politely thank your host and hostess for the
lovely time and politely say good night and politely
scram,
But when you yourself are the home team and the
gathering is under your own roof,
You haven't got a Manchurian's chance of being aloof.
If you glance at your watch it is grievous breach of
hospitality and a disgrace,

And if you are caught in the midst of a yawn you have
    to pretend you were making a face and say Come
    on everybody, let's see who can make the funniest
    face.
Then as the evening wears on you feel more and more
    like an unsuccessful gladiator,
Because all the comfortable places to sit in are being
    sat in by guests and you have to repose on the
    window sill or the chandelier or the radiator,
And also you have to run around like a specially restless
    nomadic tribe
Seeing that everybody has enough to eat and imbibe,
And somebody has always brought along a girl who
    looks like a loaf of raisin bread and doesn't know
    anybody else in the room,
And you have to go over to the corner where she is
    moping and try to disperse her gloom,
And finally at last somebody gets up and says they have
    to get back to the country or back to town again,
And you feebly say Oh it's early, don't go yet, so what
    do they do but sit down again,
And people that haven't said a word all evening begin
    to get lively and people that have been lively all
    evening get their second wind and somebody says
    Let's all go out in the kitchen and scramble some
    eggs,
And you have to look at him or her twice before you
    can convince yourself that anybody who would
    make a suggestion like that hasn't two heads or
    three legs,
And by this time the birds are twittering in the trees
    or looking in the window and saying Boo,

But nobody does anything about it and as far as I know
they're all still here, and that's the reason I say that
it is better to go and see people than to have people come and see you.

THE SAGE OF DARIEN

Upon a peak in Darien
The Sage surveys his fellow men,
Exerting to its full capacity
His preternatural sagacity.
Sore eyes and empty stomach mutiny;
The Sage confines himself to scrutiny,
Occasionally sniffing through a tube
The vapor of a bouillon cube.
Thus, all his grosser instincts chastening,
He thinks to bring the vision hastening.
The truth about his fellow men,
He hopes, will bloom within his ken.
At last appears a tiny truth,
A sliver like a baby's tooth.
Now fast it grows, it swells, it waxes,
It multiplies itself like taxes.
The ultimate truth, for what it's worth,
Crowds minor truthlets off the earth.
The Sage cries Bother! through his beard;
Says he, Exactly what I feared.
I needn't have come to Darien
To scrutinize my fellow men;
It seems I've scaled this natural steeple

To learn what I've always known about people;
To confirm through sacrifice intense
The fact that people have no sense.
People are born in pain and woe,
In woe and pain through life they go,
Harpies attend their to-and-froing,
And yet the blockheads keep on going.
Dictators tread upon their necks,
And presidents their purses vex,
Republics rob them, monarchies milk them,
Revolutions unfailingly bilk them;
Tyrants imprison them and slaughter them;
Promoters take their stocks and water them;
Statements and bills pile high around them;
Sheriffs and credit departments hound them;
By ten-ton trucks they are forced from the roads;
Every October they change their abodes;
Frequent expensive diseases smite them;
Sunbeams burn them, mosquitoes bite them;
Employers jeer at their shiny diplomas;
Advertisers insult their aromas;
People are born in pain and woe,
In woe and pain through life they go;
They have no cause at all for thanksgiving,
And yet the idiots keep on living.
Upon a peak in Darien
The Sage renounced his fellow men.
His fellow men he did renounce,
And leapt, and lit, and didn't bounce.

A CHILD'S GUIDE TO PARENTS

Children, I crave your kind forbearance;
Our topic for today is Parents.

Parents are generally found in couples,
Except when divorce their number quadruples.

Mostly they're married to each other.
The female one is called the mother.

Paternal pride being hard to edit,
The male, or father, claims the credit,

But children, hark! Your mother would rather,
When you arrived, have been your father.

At last on common ground they meet:
Their child is sweetest of the sweet.

But burst not, babe, with boastful glee;
It is themselves they praise, not thee.

The reason Father flatters thee, is —
Thou must be wonderful, aren't thou his?

And Mother admires her offspring double,
Especially after all that trouble.

The wise child handles father and mother
By playing one against the other.

Don't! cries this parent to the tot;
The opposite parent asks, Why not?

Let baby listen, nothing loth,
And work impartially on both.

In clash of wills, do not give in;
Good parents are made by discipline;

Even a backward child can foil them,
If ever careful not to spoil them.

Does Daddy his precious glasses grudge?
Remember you are the proper judge.

Does Mummy remove the scissors hence?
Fail not to chide her impudence.

Woe to the weakling lad or lass
Who lets a slight or insult pass!

Woe to the spineless, falling heir unt
To a headstrong, wayward parent!

But joy in heaping measure comes
To children whose parents are under their thumbs.

EPSTEIN, SPARE THAT YULE LOG!

When I was but a boy,
'Twas my once-a-yearly joy

To arise of a Yuletide morning,
And eagerly behold
The crimson and the gold
Of the messages the mantelpiece adorning.
There were angels, there were squires,
There were steeples, there were spires,
There were villagers, and mistletoe and holly,
There were cosy English inns
With the snow around their chins,
And I innocently thought them rather jolly.
I blush for me, but by your leave,
I'm afraid that I am still naïve.

Oh, give me an old-fashioned Christmas card,
With mistletoe galore, and holly by the yard,
With galumptious greens and gorgeous scarlets,
With crackling logs and apple-cheeked varlets,
With horses prancing down a frosty road,
And a stagecoach laden with a festive load,
And the light from the wayside windows streaming,
And a white moon rising and one star gleaming.

Departed is the time
Of Christmases sublime;
My soprano is now a mezzo-basso;
And the mantelpiece contains
The angular remains
Of a later representative Picasso.
There are circles, there are dots,
There are corners, there are spots,
There are modernistic snapshots of the city;
Or, when the artist lags,

They are livened up with gags.
You must choose between the arty and the witty.
I blush for me, but I must say
I wish you'd take them all away.

Oh, give me an old-fashioned Christmas card,
With hostlers hostling in an old inn yard,
With church bells chiming their silver notes,
And jolly red squires in their jolly red coats,
And a good fat goose by the fire that dangles,
And a few more angels and a few less angles.
Turn backward, Time, to please this bard,
And give me an old-fashioned Christmas card.

LINES WRITTEN TO CONSOLE THOSE LADIES DISTRESSED BY THE LINES "MEN SELDOM MAKE PASSES, ETC."

A girl who is bespectacled,
She may not get her nectacled,
But safety pins and bassinets
Await the girl who fascinets.

PORTRAIT OF THE ARTIST AS A PREMATURELY OLD MAN

It is common knowledge to every schoolboy and even
    every Bachelor of Arts,
That all sin is divided into two parts.

One kind of sin is called a sin of commission, and that is
very important,

And it is what you are doing when you are doing something you ortant,

And the other kind of sin is just the opposite and is
called a sin of omission and is equally bad in the
eyes of all right-thinking people, from Billy Sunday to Buddha,

And it consists of not having done something you
shuddha.

I might as well give you my opinion of these two kinds
of sin as long as, in a way, against each other we
are pitting them,

And that is, don't bother your head about sins of commission because however sinful, they must at least
be fun or else you wouldn't be committing them.

It is the sin of omission, the second kind of sin,

That lays eggs under your skin.

The way you get really painfully bitten

Is by the insurance you haven't taken out and the
checks you haven't added up the stubs of and the
appointments you haven't kept and the bills you
haven't paid and the letters you haven't written.

Also, about sins of omission there is one particularly
painful lack of beauty,

Namely, it isn't as though it had been a riotous red
letter day or night every time you neglected to do
your duty;

You didn't get a wicked forbidden thrill

Every time you let a policy lapse or forgot to pay a bill;

You didn't slap the lads in the tavern on the back and
loudly cry Whee,

Let's all fail to write just one more letter before we go
     home, and this round of unwritten letters is on me.
No, you never get any fun
Out of the things you haven't done,
But they are the things that I do not like to be amid,
Because the suitable things you didn't do give you a
     lot more trouble than the unsuitable things you
     did.
The moral is that it is probably better not to sin at all,
     but if some kind of sin you must be pursuing,
Well, remember to do it by doing rather than by not
     doing.

DRUSILLA

There was an old man of Schoharie
Who settled himself in a quarry.
And those who asked why
Got the simple reply,
"Today is the day of the soirée."

THE SPRING SITTING

Bring me a couple of highball glasses;
Fill them with sulphur and molasses;
I'm supposed to be busy as a beaver,
Instead of enjoying vernal fever.

Bring me a pin to prick me with,
Bring me a cactus to stick me with,
Bring me pinchers to pinch me with,

Bring me lynchers to lynch me with;
I'm supposed to be busy as a beaver,
Instead of enjoying vernal fever.

Burn a feather under my nose,
Hold a lighted match to my feet,
Tell me my little ones have no clothes,
And the goldfish gulp for something to eat.
Tickle my chin with a red begonia,
Ply me with aromatic ammonia,
Call me a sloth and a moral leper,
Fetch smelling salts and some cayenne pepper;
I'm supposed to be busy as a beaver
Instead of enjoying vernal fever.

I'd rather be boiled in oil than work,
I'd rather read Conan Doyle than work,
I'd rather be torn and tortured than work,
Eat peaches out of an orchard than work,
Be mean to somebody's mother than work;
In fact, do anything other than work.

It's pleasant to loll on a squashy sofa,
And when you're tired, you just roll ofa;
It's pleasant to open a thrilling book
And not to give it another look,
To open all of the windows wide
And not to bother to go outside,
To hear the robins to-and-froing,
And reflect that flowers are probably growing,
And have your corpuscles, each and every,
Wrapped in the arms of a placid revery.

Who wants to copy the busy beaver
And end in the hands of a big receiver?
Leave me alone with my vernal fever.

THE BIRD TO THE BEES

There is obviously a complete lack of understanding
  between the bee
And me.
You can't say Please
To bees.
At least, no matter with how many pleases your speech
  is bedecked,
It doesn't have any effect.
This is the simple truth that I unwilling found,
From bees following me around.
Bees cease their booming to and fro
To boom where I go;
Wherever I come,
Bees come too and hum;
Wherever I am,
There is some bee boomin' like Singin' Sam.
Night and day, day and night, under the hide of me,
There's an oh such a hungry, burning yearning to know
  why bees pay so much attention to me and upset
  me so and don't pay any attention at all to or up-
  set at all the bride of me,
Most people who are bothered by bees are bothered by
  bees only during May, June, July, August, and the
  early part of September,

But any time of the year in which the busy bees do
    not make me their business I cannot remember.
They are like the United States Mails, for the elements
    mean nothing to them,
And my garments are of what they wish to be in the
    vicinity of the hem,
And there is no sanctuary indoors,
For the room has not been built which I can enter
    without some bee which has been tuning up its
    motor, well, suddenly into life it roars,
And roses are red and violets blue,
And that's what bees ought to eat, but whatever I am
    eating they want to eat it too,
And I think that bees are what my view of life is
    owing to,
Because no bee has stung me yet but I always think
    that every bee I meet, and I meet a lot of bees, is
    going to,
And so I am ridden through life with bees in the sad-
    dle and stirrup,
So you take honey if you want, but I'll take maple
    syrup.

REFLECTIONS ON INGENUITY

Here's a good rule of thumb:
Too clever is dumb.

HOW TO TELL A QUAIL FROM A
PARTRIDGE

You all know the story of the insomniac who got into
    such a state
Because the man upstairs dropped one shoe on the floor
    at eleven o'clock and the unhappy insomniac sat
    up until breakfast time waiting for him to drop the
    mate.
Well, here I lie in the interval between the beginning
    of day and the end of night,
Waiting for a Bob White to finish saying Bob White,
And much as I should like to be one who prayeth best
    because he loveth best all things both great and
    small,
I am afraid my feeling about Bob Whites will cause my
    ranking to be reduced considerably below that of
    St. Francis and St. Paul,
Which seems a shame, because my affection would re-
    main undiminished
If he'd only say Bob White right out and get it fin-
    ished.
But this particular Bob White just says Bob,
And then goes off on some other job,
And there are you in your resentful plight,
Waiting around for him to come back and say White.
Now nobody wants to be a slavedriver or a Cossack or a
    Hessian,
But you would think it possible to get through a simple
    sentence like Bob White in one session.
If he had to cope with some complicated speech like
    Cuckoo, pu-wee, to-witta-woo, jug-jug,

Why, there'd be some excuse for remembering in the
middle of it that he had to go see a man about a
bug.
You could possibly sympathize with him, you think,
For hesitating over something silly like Spink spank
spink;
And yes, you say to yourself as you toss on your sleep-
less pillow,
No self-respecting bird could be expected not to break
down halfway through such a humiliating speech
as Willow tit-willow tit-willow,
But this isn't at all the same.
What are you going to do with a bird that can't even
remember its own name?
If you were the King of Italy and you asked a man his
name and he said Benito and then came back half
an hour later and added Mussolini,
Would you ask him please to go ahead and form a Fas-
cist State or would you tell him to tell it to
Sweeney?
Well, I hope these bitter words of mine will have some
effect in inducing Bob Whites to memorize their
parts with all their might,
Or at least that from now on they'll go out only in
couples, one to remember to say Bob and the
other to remember to say White.

THEY DON'T SPEAK ENGLISH IN PARIS

I wish that I could get in line
And shout the praise of Gertrude Stein.

In any high-class hullabaloo
I rather like to holler too;
I hate like anything to miss
Swelling the roar of Ah! Boom! Siss!
And most particularly when
The cheers are led by famous men.
The fault I'm sure is solely mine,
But I cannot root for Gertrude Stein.
For Gertrude Stein I cannot root;
I cannot blow a single toot;
I must preserve a dreary silence,
Though doomed thereby to durance vilence.
I'm fond of women, also wine,
But not the song of Gertrude Stein.
No laurels can I pass, alas,
To pigeons on the grass, alas.
Oh woefully must I decline
To dance in the street for Gertrude Stein.
O Gertrude, Gertrude, is it me?
Couldn't it possibly be thee?
Not in the face of all the roses
Awarded thee by them who knowses.
From Walla Walla to the Rhine
Carillons clang for Gertrude Stein,
Rung not by nitwit nincompoops,
But geniuses in fervent groups.
Those pens of talent most divine
Scratch noisiest for Gertrude Stein;
Neglecting all their personal muttons,
They genuflect to Tender Buttons.
Why must I grunt, a lonely swine,
Rejecting the pearls of Gertrude Stein?

Why can't I praise in cataracts
Her Four such Saints in Three such Acts?
Four Saints, Three Acts; Three Acts, in fact
The Acts get a Saint-and-a-third an act,
And Lizzie Borden took three axe
And gave her mother tongue forty whacks,
And a hundred eminent artistic figures
Swallowed the woodpile including the nigures.
I prefer to wade through Rasselas
To pigeons on the grass, alas.
The English language is better as language
Than spattered like a lettuce and mayonnaise sanguage,
So let those who will read Alice B. Toklas,
And I'll take the complete works of Shakespeare and a
    box of chocolas.

THE STRANGE CASE OF THE GIRL O' MR. SPONSOON'S DREAMS

Once upon a time there was a man named Mr. Spon-
    soon who was highly ineffectual.

∽

He always looked as if he were growing a mustache.

∽

His singing voice was pretty fair except for the high
    notes.

∽

Oh yes, and the low notes, too.

∽

One day he was driving along the street when he saw
    a beautiful girl.

∽

My, what a beautiful girl, said Mr. Sponsoon, I wish I
knew her name.

∞

If I asked her her name, said Mr. Sponsoon, she might
think me a brazen cad.

∞

But if I don't know her name, she will go out of my life
forever.

∞

Mr. Sponsoon thought and thought.

∞

Suppose I run over her gently, he thought at last.

∞

With one wheel, say.

∞

Certainly with no more than two.

∞

Then I can read her name in the morning paper and all
will be hotsy-totsy.

∞

Mr. Sponsoon pointed his car at the beautiful girl.

∞

The beautiful girl leaped like a thoroughbred gazelle.

∞

Mr. Sponsoon chased her for seven blocks and never
laid a wheel on her.

∞

In the middle of the eighth block she stopped to
moisten her finger on account of a run in her
stocking.

∞

Mr. Sponsoon read in the morning paper that her name was Shella Schminck and she was in Percy's Hospital.

⁂

So he went to the Mercy Hospital and asked for Stella Smith.

⁂

To the girl o' his dreams he explained his little stratagem.

⁂

Girl o' my dreams, I had to know your name, said Mr. Sponsoon, avoiding high notes and low notes.

⁂

Say you forgive me, girl o' my dreams.

⁂

Say all is hotsy-totsy.

⁂

The girl o' Mr. Sponsoon's dreams said all was far from hotsy-totsy.

⁂

All was coldsy-toldsy, said the girl o' Mr. Sponsoon's dreams.

⁂

Mr. Sponsoon joined the Foreign Legion, but was soon expelled because he admitted he liked it.

⁂

When last heard of, he was borrowing a burnt cork from Amos and Andy.

⁂

He said he had decided to steal into Rome as an Ethiopian spy.

· 145 ·

Ah woe, woe, woe, man was created to live by the sweat
of his brow,

And it doesn't make any difference if your brow was
moist yesterday and the day before, you've still got
to get it moist again right now,

And you know deep in your heart that you will have to
continue keeping it dewy

Right up to the time that somebody at the club says, I
suppose we ought to go to what's-his-name's funeral, who won the fifth at Bowie?

That's a nasty outlook to face,

But it's what you get for belonging to the human race.

So far as I know, mankind is the only section of creation

That is doomed to either pers- or ex-piration.

Look at the birds flying around, and listen to them as
their voices in song they hoist;

No wonder they sing so much, they haven't got any
brows, and if they had they couldn't be bothered
keeping them moist.

And bees don't do anything either, bees just have a
reputation for industry because they are sharp
enough to buzz,

And people hear a bee buzzing and don't realize that
buzzing isn't any trouble for a bee so they think it
is doing more than it actually does,

So next time you are about to expend some enthusiasm
on the bee's wonderful industrial powers,

Just remember that that wonderful bee would die
laughing if you asked it to change places with you

and get *its* brow moist while you went around
    spending the day smelling flowers.
Oh yes, and the flowers, they seem to get along all right
    without being overactive,
All they do is sit around looking attractive,
And furthermore, if you can believe all you hear,
They only get up energy enough to do that about once
    a year.
Thus we see that if you are botany
Your life is just an everlasting spell of pleasant monot-
    ony,
But if you are humanity, it is far from so,
And that is why I exclaim Woe woe woe,
Because I don't see much good in being the highest
    form of life
If all you get out of it is a brow moist from perpetual
    struggle and strife.
Indeed sometimes when my brow is particularly moist
    I think I would rather be a humble amœba
Than Solomon in all his glory entertaining the Queen
    of Sheba.

THE OYSTER

The oyster's a confusing suitor;
It's masc., and fem., and even neuter.
But whether husband, pal or wife
It leads a painless sort of life.
I'd like to be an oyster, say,
In August, June, July or May.

LISTEN . . .

There is a knocking in the skull,
An endless silent shout
Of something beating on a wall,
And crying, Let me out.

That solitary prisoner
Will never hear reply,
No comrade in eternity
Can hear the frantic cry.

No heart can share the terror
That haunts his monstrous dark;
The light that filters through the chinks
No other eye can mark.

When flesh is linked with eager flesh,
And words run warm and full,
I think that he is loneliest then,
The captive in the skull.

Caught in a mesh of living veins,
In cell of padded bone,
He loneliest is when he pretends
That he is not alone.

We'd free the incarcerate race of man
That such a doom endures
Could only you unlock my skull,
Or I creep into yours.

CARLOTTA

There was an old man in a trunk,
Who inquired of his wife, "Am I drunk?"
She replied with regret,
"I'm afraid so, my pet,"
And he answered, "It's just as I thunk."

PRETTY HALCYON DAYS

How pleasant to sit on the beach,
On the beach, on the sand, in the sun,
With ocean galore within reach,
And nothing at all to be done!
No letters to answer,
No bills to be burned,
No work to be shirked,
No cash to be earned.
It is pleasant to sit on the beach
With nothing at all to be done.

How pleasant to look at the ocean,
Democratic and damp; indiscriminate;
It fills me with noble emotion
To think I am able to swim in it.
To lave in the wave,
Majestic and chilly,
Tomorrow I crave;
But today it is silly.
It is pleasant to look at the ocean;
Tomorrow, perhaps, I shall swim in it.

How pleasant to gaze at the sailors,
As their sailboats they manfully sail
With the vigor of vikings and whalers
In the days of the viking and whale.
They sport on the brink
Of the shad and the shark;
If it's windy they sink;
If it isn't, they park.
It is pleasant to gaze at the sailors,
To gaze without having to sail.

How pleasant the salt anæsthetic
Of the air and the sand and the sun;
Leave the earth to the strong and athletic,
And the sea to adventure upon.
But the sun and the sand
No contractor can copy;
We lie in the land
Of the lotus and poppy;
We vegetate, calm and æsthetic,
On the beach, on the sand, in the sun.

I'LL TAKE A BROMIDE, PLEASE

Alas that it should be my duty
To explain to the younger generation that beauty is not
    always truth nor truth beauty,
Because Good Gracious,
Half the time truth is very unsightly indeed and beauty
    is very mendacious,
So hurry up, Intelligent Youth,

And make up your mind whether you want beauty or
    truth,
Because I take my unwilling oath
That you can't have both,
And if you vote for truth I think you will someday look
    on me with gratitude
For having called your attention to the merits of the
    platitude.
No paradox of Mr. Chesterton's ever contained the
    amount of validity
Contained in the simple statement that It's not the
    heat, it's the humidity;
Wilde and his epigrams are shown up as brilliant bores
Before the unpretentious penetration of the comment
    that It never rains but it pours.
Did Swift ever say anything as keen as that the best way
    to keep it from raining is to carry an umbrella?
Did Plato ever rise to the heights of exclaiming that
    he believed mosquitoes were really attracted by
    citronella?
Shakespeare himself never said anything as true
As that you can stand on a corner and a hundred trolley
    cars and taxis will go by when you don't want
    them but there isn't one in sight when you do.
Ah, Youth, Youth!
It is well to remember that the mighty platitude is
    made up of little drops of experience, little grains
    of truth.
Do not seek to acquire the wisdom of the ages
From the philosophers and sages;
You will not find it in any old ism or any new ism;
Truth doesn't lie in the well, it lies in the truism;

So if truth is the one thing you are determined to keep
    in sight,
Well, to put the whole thing in a nutshell, where it
    probably belongs anyhow, if it's trite, it's right.

ODE TO C. B. E., PRACTICALLY THE ONLY NEW MALE CHILD I KNOW OF

Hail, third-born infant of my friend,
Thou rosy extra dividend!
What mirth enlivens thy vicinity,
Thou handsome example of masculinity!
Thou rugged atom, thou hairless he-man,
Potential President or G-man!
Thy parents said they didn't care
Were thou an heiress or an heir.
"It's all the same to us," they cried.
Good gracious, how thy parents lied!
Thy father bounded like a squirrel
When scientists pronounced thee virile;
Thy mother danced upon her cot
When told a daughter thou wert not;
Thy sisters' eyes with glee did glister
At doing without another sister;
And o'er Manhattan, from river to river,
There ran a thrill, there ran a quiver.
The buildings rocked, the bridges trembled,
As males in milling hordes assembled;
A million men, agog and eager,
The lucky hospital did beleaguer
To pop their eyes and crane their necks

At the new addition to their sex,
As well they might, to calm their fears;
Thou wert the first in years and years,
And fathers gazed in wild despair
At daughters, daughters everywhere.
Oh, late and early, night and morn,
Nothing but girls was being born;
Then, as the scornfulest of affronts,
They started coming five at once.
And men were filled with thickening gloom
At prospects of their sex's doom;
The future fraught with meek surrender
To the overwhelming feminine gender;
A world of regnant Amazons,
Perkinses, Roosevelts, and Dionnes.
But now they glimpse in thine arrival
A fighting chance for man's survival.
All hail the man who had a son!
Others can do what he has done!
And hail to thee, thou hopeful token
Of feminine fetters finally broken!
Yea, thanks to thee, this spinning ball
May be a man's world after all.

DING DONG, TOOT TOOT, ALL ABOARD

If there is one group of professional men that more
    than any other group of professional men itself to
    me endears,
It is the honorable brotherhood of locomotive engi-
    neers.

They sit at the helm of their great big panting iron
    horses,
And steer them as accurately as the stars in their
    courses,
And if they start or stop with a jerk while you are in
    the diner so that your clothes get sprinkled with
    ice cream and syrup and coffee and waffle,
They feel awful.
They may not be quite sure when to wear full dress and
    when to wear Tuxedoes,
But they are never in doubt about what to do when the
    signals change or they run over torpedoes,
And nobody is prompter
In the face of hell, high water and sub-zero thermomter,
But in spite of being so punctilious,
They are not the least bit supercilious.
It seems to be as natural for a locomotive engineer to
    be friendly as it is for the voice of the newsreel to
    make inane puns or a duck to say Quack quack,
And when you drive the baby down to see the train go
    by and say Look at the train, baby, wave at the
    nice locomotive engineer, and the baby waves, why,
    the locomotive engineer waves right back.
Long have I wondered why a locomotive engineer
    should be so much nicer than an ambassador or
    a novelist or a banker or a third-baseman or a
    quartermaster or a lancer,
And at last I think I've got the answer.
During their boyhood years
All nice little boys want to grow up to be locomotive
    engineers,
But as they approach maturity,

The ambitions of all except the very nicest lose their
    purity,
And only in the breasts of the crème de la crème de la
    crème
Still burns the hard, gemlike flame,
And that's the reason why locomotive engineers num-
    ber in their ranks no cads or poltroons or snobs or
    hoi pollois,
Because their ranks are recruited only from the nicest
    of all the nice little boys.

HOME, 99⁴⁴⁄₁₀₀% SWEET HOME

Most of the time, oh most of the time,
I like to sit at home,
With a good fire, and a good chair,
And a good detective tome.
What can a man, can a family man
Ask in the way of cheer
More than a pipe, and a reading lamp,
And a modest mug of beer?
Most of the time, the wealth of the Indies
Wouldn't tempt me to blowouts or shindies.

But once in a while,
Oh, once in a while,
It's pleasant to paint the town,
To frolic and revel,
A regular devil,
And do the evening brown.
To buy an orchid, or maybe two,

And woo the way that you used to woo,
To press the loot from the babies' banks
On waiters who fail to murmur thanks,
To dine and wine and dance and sup,
And ride in a cab till the sun comes up,
And to feel thereafter, in sundry ways,
Simply awful for days and days.
Home is heaven and orgies are vile,
But I like an orgy, once in a while.

Home is the place, oh home is the place
That no place else is like,
So who would freeze in the South, like Byrd,
Or discover peaks, like Pike?
Who so animal, who so low
As to pant for the Great White Way?
Who would give up a night at home
For one in a cabaret?
Most of the time I'd swim to Australia
As soon as engage in a Saturnalia.

But once in a while,
Oh once in a while,
It's pleasant to loop the loop,
To daringly seize
The flying trapeze
With a cry of Allez-oop!
To jump the rails, kick over the traces,
To go on the town and visit places,
Sit ten at a table meant for two,
And choke on smoke as you used to do,
To tread the floor with the dancing bears,

They on your feet, and you on theirs,
To have flings at things that philosophers true shun,
And undermine your constitue-shun.
Home is heaven and orgies are vile,
But you need an orgy, once in a while.

HOME THOUGHTS FROM LITTLE MOOSE

I

O hills and rills of Uncle Sam,
O Adirondacks, here I am!
I like your lakes, I like your woods,
I like your line of verdant goods,
I like your rosy-toed Aurora,
I like your fauna and your flora,
And most of all, of this be sure,
I like your average temperature.
At ninety-five I'd have no use
For Panther Lake or Little Moose,
But at a pleasant sixty-nine
I'm glad to say I like them fine.
I like to haunt their leafy shelters
And chuckle while the city swelters.
You splendid folk of spirit brotherly,
I blame you not for feeling otherly.
Nobody more than I admires
The kindly deeds of Bishop Stires,
The ditto deeds of Ditto Manning,
The generous hand, the thoughtful planning
Nobody less than I resists

The pleadings of philanthropists.
But ask me not to divvy up
The contents of this cooling cup,
Or advocate with Doctor Reiland
An Adirondack Coney Island.

II

O Adirondacks, here am I,
Myself I'm happy to be by.
Let those who think me rude to chortle
Remember that I'm only mortal;
Let them deduce, with rare acumen,
That, being mortal, I am human.
Yea, let them feel, and rightly feel,
That, being human, I'm a heel.
Although there's room for thousands more
Along this air-conditioned shore,
I do not feel inclined to share
Condition, shore or even air,
And I would rather not divide
The view of yonder mountain side.
The birds that haunt that wooded shelf,
I'll listen to them by myself.
A double joy, a double pride,
Is that which others are denied.
You know the Manger and the Terrier? —
In other words, the less the merrier.

LONG LIVE DELAYS OF ANCIENT ROME

Mankind in the course of countless centuries has acted
in one theory

Of which I am very, very weory,

But it has been generally accepted ever since some talkative go-getter first heaved himself up out of the primeval ooze and slime

And remarked to all the rest of the amœbas or mudpuppies or whatever they were who were probably perfectly happy where they were, Come on up out of the primeval ooze and slime, all you amœbas or mudpuppies or whatever you are and don't procrastinate because I've just figured out that Procrastination is the thief of time.

And to this very day, when thanks to Professor Einstein we don't even know what Time is, or whether there is any Time, or whether Time is Space or whether Time and Space are Amos and Andy,

People keep on saying that Procrastination is the thief of it, just as they did when Time was something perfectly definite in the days of Ben Hur and Tristram Shandy.

The truth is that the thieves are a couple of other thieves, and one of them is Employment,

And the other is Enjoyment,

Because the hands of the clock whirl around like a revolving door in the rush hour that has just been greased

When you are very busy or very pleased,

And it seems to me that when you are deprived of a sizeable quantity of time like that without even a chance to say hello,

Well, if that isn't stealing, I don't know.

So instead of talking about procrastination, all the people who declare that to have any time stolen they cannot afford,

Why, to be perfectly logical and make their time last
    as long as possible they ought to concentrate on
    being constantly bored,
Which condition, if you will take the word of one who
    much among them digs and delves,
They might easily attain by talking to themselves.
Far from being the thief of Time, Procrastination is the
    king of it,
And therefore I sing of it.
The really accomplished procrastinator can conquer the
    minutes and hours as easily as dragons were con-
    quered by Sir Launcelot,
Because he can regulate the flow so as to have just a
    little time when just a little is enough and a lot
    when he wauncelot.
After he has mastered the technique
He can make a nasty week last a minute or a pleasant
    minute last a week.
So Hail to thee, Procrastination, I would I had the pen
    and tongue of a British lecturer to describe thy
    numerous attractions,
And I will always be faithful to thee if thou wilt prom-
    ise to have nothing to do with any of the people
    whose railroads I ride on or with whom I have
    business transactions.

THE DUCK

Behold the duck.
It does not cluck.
A cluck it lacks.

It quacks.
It is specially fond
Of a puddle or pond.
When it dines or sups,
It bottoms ups.

THE CLEAN PLATTER

Some singers sing of ladies' eyes,
And some of ladies' lips,
Refined ones praise their ladylike ways,
And coarse ones hymn their hips.
The Oxford Book of English Verse
Is lush with lyrics tender;
A poet, I guess, is more or less,
Preoccupied with gender.
Yet I, though custom call me crude,
Prefer to sing in praise of food.

Food,
Yes, food,
Just any old kind of food.
Pooh for the cook,
And pooh for the price!
Some of it's nicer but all of it's nice.
Pheasant is pleasant, of course,
And terrapin, too, is tasty,
Lobster I freely endorse,
In pâté or patty or pasty.
But there's nothing the matter with butter,
And nothing the matter with jam,

And the warmest of greetings I utter
To the ham and the yam and the clam.
For they're food,
All food,
And I think very highly of food.
Though I'm broody at times
When bothered by rhymes,
I brood
On food.

Some painters paint the sapphire sea,
And some the gathering storm.
Others portray young lambs at play,
But most, the female form.
'Twas trite in that primeval dawn
When painting got its start,
That a lady with her garments on
Is Life, but is she Art?
By undraped nymphs
I am not wooed;
I'd rather painters painted food.

Food,
Just food,
Just any old kind of food.
Let it be sour
Or let it be sweet,
As long as you're sure it is something to eat.
Go purloin a sirloin, my pet,
If you'd win a devotion incredible;
And asparagus tips vinaigrette,
Or anything else that is edible.

Bring salad or sausage or scrapple,
A berry or even a beet.
Bring an oyster, an egg, or an apple,
As long as it's something to eat.
If it's food,
It's food;
Never mind what kind of food.
Through thick and through thin
I am constantly in
The mood
For food.

ASIDE TO HUSBANDS

What do you do when you've wedded a girl all legal
    and lawful,
And she goes around saying she looks awful?
When she makes deprecatory remarks about her format,
And claims that her hair looks like a doormat?
When she swears that the complexion of which you are
    so fond
Looks like the bottom of a dried-up pond?
When she says her ankles are the same as her legs,
And both are like kegs?
When she for whom your affection is not the least like
    Plato's
Compares her waist to a badly tied sack of potatoes?
When she thinks that every hour is the hour at which
    avoirdupois begins,
And keeps discovering nonexistent double and triple
    chins?

When she regrets her mouth,

And frowns at her nose for pointing North instead of South?

Oh, who wouldn't rather be on a flimsy bridge with a hungry lion at one end and a hungry tiger at the other end and hungry crocodiles underneath

Than confronted by their dearest making remarks about her own appearance through clenched teeth?

Oh, who wouldn't rather drown in the deepest ocean or crackle in the most furious fire,

Than be in a position where if you say Yes darling, you are told you don't love her any more, and if you say No darling you are told you are a hypocritical liar?

Why won't they believe that the reason they find themselves the mother of your children is because you think of all the looks in the world, their looks are the nicest?

Why must we continue to be thus constantly ordealed and crisised?

I think it high time these hoity-toity ladies were made to realize that when they impugn their face and their ankles and their waist

They are thereby insultingly impugning their tasteful husbands' impeccable taste.

UNCALLED-FOR EPITAPH:
THE SPORTS ANNOUNCER

"Oh boy! I'm down — I'm up — in Heaven! —
"The Nine Apostles — No, it's Seven! —

"Oh boy! St. Peter's got the ball! —
"I'm wrong, it's Luke — No, wait, it's Paul!"
Good old Graham!
Always the Saham.

HEARTS OF GOLD
or
A GOOD EXCUSE IS WORSE THAN NONE

There are some people who are very resourceful
At being remorseful,
And who apparently feel that the best way to make
    friends
Is to do something terrible and then make amends.
They come to your party and make a great hit with
    your Victorian aunt and with her freely mingle,
And suddenly after another drink they start a lot of
    double entendre the entendre of which is unfortu-
    nately not double but single,
And if you say anything to them they take umbrage,
And later when you are emptying the ash trays before
    going to bed you find them under the sofa where
    they have crept for a good night's slumbrage.
Then next day they are around intoning apologies
With all the grace and conviction of a high-paid choir
    intoning doxologies.
There are people in every group
Who will jog your elbow at table just when you are
    lifting a spoonful of very hot soup,
Or at a musicale or something while you're listening
    to a ravishing obbligato

Will forget their cigarettes and burn a hole in your
　　clothes the size of a medium-sized tomato.
And then you are presented with a lot of form-fitting
　　apologies
Quite good enough, I am sure, for inclusion in one of
　　the higher-class anthologies.
Everybody says these people have hearts of gold,
But nevertheless they're always talking when you're
　　putting, or splashing mud on you from their car,
　　or giving you a cold,
And they are always sure that today you don't mind
　　their inflicting on you any sorrow,
Because they'll give you so much pleasure when they
　　smilingly apologize tomorrow,
But I myself would rather have a rude word from some-
　　one who has done me no harm
Than a graceful letter from the Prince of Wales saying
　　he's sorry he broke my arm.

ADVENTURES OF ISABEL

Isabel met an enormous bear,
Isabel, Isabel, didn't care;
The bear was hungry, the bear was ravenous,
The bear's big mouth was cruel and cavernous.
The bear said, Isabel, glad to meet you,
How do, Isabel, now I'll eat you!
Isabel, Isabel, didn't worry,
Isabel didn't scream or scurry.
She washed her hands and she straightened her hair up,
Then Isabel quietly ate the bear up.

Once in a night as black as pitch
Isabel met a wicked old witch.
The witch's face was cross and wrinkled,
The witch's gums with teeth were sprinkled.
Ho ho, Isabel! the old witch crowed,
I'll turn you into an ugly toad!
Isabel, Isabel, didn't worry,
Isabel didn't scream or scurry,
She showed no rage and she showed no rancor,
But she turned the witch into milk and drank her.

Isabel met a hideous giant,
Isabel continued self-reliant.
The giant was hairy, the giant was horrid,
He had one eye in the middle of his forehead.
Good morning Isabel, the giant said,
I'll grind your bones to make my bread.
Isabel, Isabel, didn't worry,
Isabel didn't scream or scurry.
She nibbled the zwieback that she always fed off,
And when it was gone, she cut the giant's head off.

Isabel met a troublesome doctor,
He punched and he poked till he really shocked her.
The doctor's talk was of coughs and chills
And the doctor's satchel bulged with pills.
The doctor said unto Isabel,
Swallow this, it will make you well.
Isabel, Isabel, didn't worry,
Isabel didn't scream or scurry.
She took those pills from the pill concocter,
And Isabel calmly cured the doctor.

THE CAMEL

The camel has a single hump;
The dromedary, two;
Or else the other way around.
I'm never sure. Are you?

THE EVENING OUT

You have your hat and coat on and she says she will
be right down,
And you hope so because it is getting late and you are
dining on the other side of town,
And you are pretty sure she can't take long,
Because when you left her she already looked as neat
as a Cole Porter song,
And so goes ten minutes, and then fifteen minutes, and
then half an hour,
And you listen for the sound of water running because
you suspect she may have gone back for an extra
bath or a shower,
Or maybe she decided her hair was a mess and is now
shampooing it,
But whatever she is up to, she is a long time doing it,
And finally she comes down and says she is sorry she
couldn't find the right lipstick, that's why she was
so slow,
And you look at her and she looks marvelous but not a
bit more marvelous than she did when you left
her forty-five minutes ago,

And you tell her she looks ravishing and she says No,
   she is a sight,
And you reflect that you are now an hour late, but at
   any rate she is now groomed for the rest of the
   night,
So you get to your destination and there's the ladies'
   dressing room and before you know it she's in it,
But she says she'll be back in a minute,
And so she is, but not to tarry,
No, only to ask you for her bag, which she has forgot-
   ten she had asked you to carry,
So you linger in the lobby
And wish you had a nice portable hobby,
And when she eventually reappears she doesn't apolo-
   gize, but glances at you as if you were Bluebeard
   or Scrooge,
And says why didn't you tell her she had on too much
   rouge?
And you look to see what new tint she has acquired,
And she looks just the same as she did before she re-
   tired,
So you dine, and reach the theater in time for the
   third act, and then go somewhere to dance and
   sup,
And she says she looks like a scarecrow, she has to go
   straighten up,
So then you don't see her for quite a long time,
But at last you see her for a moment when she comes
   out to ask if you will lend her a dime,
The moral of all which is that you will have just as
   much of her company and still save considerable
   on cover charges and beverages and grub

If instead of taking her out on the town, you settle her
        in a nice comfortable dressing room and then go
        off and spend the evening at the Club.

SEPTEMBER MORN

Oh, what in the world could be more fun
Than to have your holiday over and done;
Than to stand in a rural railway station
With fifty weeks till your next vacation!
Ah me, what jovial words are spoken
When you find the suitcase handle is broken.
You juggle golf bags and tennis rackets,
And ludicrous bulging paper packets,
You count your paraphernalia twice
From the children themselves to their milk and ice.
A whistle announces the train is coming;
You drop the children's portable plumbing;
The train draws up with a jerk and a wiggle
From the engineer's convulsive giggle,
And every window flattens the nose
Of a passenger reveling in your woes.
The steps are as steep as next year's taxes
And wicked as Jukeses and Kallikakses.
Heave up the bags, the ice, the milk,
Heave up your struggling youthful ilk!
Heave up, heave up, and keep on heaving;
This good old train will soon be leaving.
The grim conductor, watch in hand,
Glares angrily on your hapless band.
Oh when was order e'er restored

By disgusted cries of All aboard?
This luggage on the platform piled
May well conceal a favorite child.
Conductor, cease your cry disgusted;
Distracted parents can't be trusted,
In times of stress they have been known
To ship their offspring off alone;
Not unprotected, not at large,
But in the kind conductor's charge.
Farewell, farewell to the sand and foam,
You are getting yourself and your family home.
Oh, I think there is no such capital fun
But having your teeth out one by one.

MR. BARCALOW'S BREAKDOWN

Once there was a man, and he was named Mr. Bar-
        calow, to be exact,
And he prided himself on his tact,
And he said, One thing about an apple, it may have a
        worm in it, and one thing about a chimney, it
        may have soot in it,
But one thing about my mouth, I never put my foot
        in it.
Whenever Mr. Barcalow entered a community
He inquired of his host and hostess what topics he
        could discuss with impunity,
So no matter beside whom he was deposited,
Why, he could talk to them without disturbing any
        skeletons that should have been kept closeted,
But one dire day he went to visit some friends,

And he started asking tactful questions about untact-
ful conversational trends,

And his host said that here was one place that Mr. Barcalow wouldn't need his tact,

Because taboos and skeletons were what everybody
there lacked,

And his hostess said, Oh yes, but you'd better steer
away from education when you talk to the Senator,

Because somebody said his seventeen-year-old nephew
would have to burn down the schoolhouse to get
out of the third grade and his nephew overheard
them and did burn down the schoolhouse, including the music teacher and the janitor,

And his host said, Oh yes, and if you talk about love
and marriage to Mrs. Musker don't be surprised
if her eye sort of wanders,

Because her daughter is the one who had the divorce
suit with thirty-seven co-responders,

And Mr. Barcalow said, Well, can I talk about sports;

And his hostess said, Well maybe you'd better not because Louise's sister, the queer one, was asked to
resign from the club because she went out to play
moonlight tennis in shorts; and Mr. Barcalow said
That's not so terrible is it, everybody wears shorts;
and his hostess said, Yes, but she forgot the shorts;

So Mr. Barcalow said Well then, what about the
weather?

And his host said Well, that's what we used to discuss
when we got together,

But it has recently become a pleasure we must defer,

Because Jane's Aunt Julia is here from California and

she seems to think every remark about the weather
　　is a personal affront to her.
So Mr. Barcalow said, The hell with you all, and went
　　upstairs and packed,
And that was the last that was ever heard of Mr. Bar-
　　calow and his tact.

THE BIG TENT UNDER THE ROOF

Noises new to sea and land
Issue from the circus band.
Each musician looks like mumps
From blowing umpah umpah umps.

Lovely girls in spangled pants
Ride on gilded elephants.
Elephants are useful friends,
They have handles on both ends;
They hold each other's hindmost handles
And flee from mice and Roman candles.
Their hearts are gold, their hides are emery,
And they have a most tenacious memory.

Notice also, girls and boys,
The circus horses' avoirdupois.
Far and wide the wily scouts
Seek these snow-white stylish stouts.
Calmer steeds were never found
Unattached to a merry-go-round.
Equestriennes prefer to jump
Onto horses pillow-plump.

Equestriennes will never ride
As other people do, astride.
They like to balance on one foot,
And wherever they get, they won't stay put.
They utter frequent whoops and yips,
And have the most amazing hips.
Pink seems to be their favorite color,
And very few things are very much duller.

Yet I for one am more than willing
That everything should be less thrilling.
My heart and lungs both bound and balk
When high-wire walkers start to walk.
They ought to perish, yet they don't;
Some fear they will, some fear they won't.

I lack the adjectives, verbs and nouns
To do full justice to the clowns.
Their hearts are constantly breaking, I hear,
And who am I to interfere?

Still, I could interfere for weeks
With those who come to mock the freaks.
Buzzards that gloat on Nature's denials
Buy souvenirs at murder trials.

Am I making an acorn out of a quercus?
Guess again, please. Let's go to the circus!

THE TURKEY

There is nothing more perky
Than a masculine turkey.
When he struts he struts
With no ifs or buts.
When his face is apoplectic
His harem grows hectic,
And when he gobbles
Their universe wobbles.

KIND OF AN ODE TO DUTY

O Duty,
Why hast thou not the visage of a sweetie or a cutie?
Why glitter thy spectacles so ominously?
Why art thou clad so abominously?
Why art thou so different from Venus
And why do thou and I have so few interests mutually
    in common between us?
Why art thou fifty per cent martyr
And fifty-one per cent Tartar?

Why is it thy unfortunate wont
To try to attract people by calling on them either to
    leave undone the deeds they like, or to do the
    deeds they don't?
Why art thou so like an April post-mortem
Or something that died in the ortumn?
Above all, why dost thou continue to hound me?
Why art thou always albatrossly hanging around me?

Thou so ubiquitous,
And I so iniquitous.
I seem to be the one person in the world thou art per-
petually preaching at who or to who;
Whatever looks like fun, there art thou standing be-
tween me and it, calling yoo-hoo.
O Duty, Duty!
How noble a man should I be hadst thou the visage of
a sweetie or a cutie!
But as it is thou art so much forbiddinger than a Wode-
house hero's forbiddingest aunt
That in the words of the poet, When Duty whispers
low, Thou must, this erstwhile youth replies, I
just can't.

THE LIFE OF THE PARTY

Lily, there isn't a thing you lack,
Your effect is simply stunning.
But Lily, your gown is low in the back,
So conduct yourself with cunning.
Some of your charm is charm of face,
But some of your charm is spinal;
Losing your looks is no disgrace,
But losing your poise is final.
Ridicule's name is Legion,
So look to your dorsal region.

For Artie,
Old Artie,
The life of the party,

Is practically perfect tonight;
He's prettily, properly tight;
He's never appeared so bright.
Have you ever seen Artie
Enliven a party? .
You've never seen Artie —
Why Lord love a duck!
At present old Artie is running amuck.
There's a wink in his eye
And a smile on his lips
For the matron he tickles,
The waiter he trips.
There's a rubber cigar,
And a smoking-room jest,
To melt the reserve
Of the clerical guest.
There's a pin for the man who stoops over,
And a little trained flea for Rover.
So Lily, beware of your back!
More daring than duller and older blades,
Artie is hot on the track.
I've noticed him eying your shoulderblades.
And maybe it's salad,
And maybe it's ice,
But I fear he has planned
Some amusing device,
For the laughter is slack
And he's taking it hard —
He's eying your back —
And Artie's a card —
He's forming a plan —
May I fetch you a shawl?

That inventive young man —
There is one in the hall.
Though your back is divine
In its natural state,
May I curtain your spine? —
Dear Heaven, I'm late!
Aren't you glad that you came to the party?
And weren't you amused by Artie?

Horace, the moment that you appeared,
I admired your manly beauty,
But I feel that a word about your beard
Is only my bounden duty.
Your tailor's craft is a dandy's dream,
Your suavity leaves me lyrical,
But escaping tonight with your self-esteem
Will require a minor miracle.
Fun is a gay deceiver,
So look to your kingly beaver.

For Artie,
Old Artie,
The life of the party,
Is hitting his stride tonight.
No bushel obscures his light.
He's knocking them left and right.
Have you ever seen Artie
Enliven a party?
You've never seen Artie —
My lad, you're in luck,
For Artie, old Artie, is running amuck.

At Artie's approach
Lesser wags droop.
Have you seen the tin roach
He drops in your soup?
Is a spoon in your pocket?
Or gum in your chair?
It's Artie, old Artie,
Who magicked them there.
And of those who complain, there's a rumor
That they're lacking in sense of humor.
So Horace, beware of your beard!
I scent some fantastic flubdubbery!
Old Artie has just disappeared
And I've noticed him eying your shrubbery.
And maybe it's syrup,
And maybe it's mice,
But I fear he has planned
Some amusing device.
His conceptions are weird,
And nothing is barred —
He was eying your beard —
And Artie's a card —
When Artie returns,
The fun will begin —
May I fetch you a bag
To put on your chin?
Just a small paper bag
To envelop the bait?
For Artie's a wag —
Dear Heaven, I'm late!
Aren't you glad that you came to the party?
And weren't you amused by Artie?

AIMEE McPHERSON

Said Aimee McPherson to Barbara Hutton,
How do you get a marriage to button?
You'll have to ask some other person,
Said Barbara Hutton to Aimee McPherson.

OH, PLEASE DON'T GET UP!

There is one form of life to which I unconditionally
surrender,
Which is the feminine gender.
Like lightning and thunder, women are awe-inspiring
natural phenomena,
And they have a custom which many men might well
adopt, which is to gird themselves in devices that
reduce or at least repress their abdomena,
And they have a traditional rite which is handed down
from mother to daughter,
Which is that they always have to wash their face with
cold cream instead of water.
Also, I think there must be some great difference in the
way men and women are built,
Because women walk around all day wearing shoes that
a man would break his neck the first step he took
in them because where a man's shoe has a heel a
woman's shoe has a stilt.
Yes, certainly a man shod like a woman would just have
to sit down all day, and yet my land!
Women not only don't have to sit, but prefer to stand,
Because their pleasure in standing up is exquisite,

Especially on a visit,
Because at first they will sit in a chair,
And their heart may be in the highlands, but it certainly isn't there,
And their conversation is unspontaneous,
And their topics are trifling and miscellaneous,
But finally, after an uncomfortable while,
Their faces brighten with the well-I-must-be-running-along-now smile,
And they get to their feet and the front door,
And the Old Mother of Waters surges over the levee with a roar,
Because the proportions of feminine social chitchat are constant, always;
One part of sitting down in the sitting room to four parts standing up saying good-by in foyers and hallways,
Which is why I think that when it comes to physical prowess,
Why woman is a wow, or should I say a wowess?

THE MARKETEERS

Get out of the way, little boys on skates!
Out of the way, little girls with dates!
Clear the road, ye dogs and cats,
And ye agèd roués in toppers and spats!
Ye efts and newts, no more be seen,
And O! ye traffic lights, shine green!
Two jolly marketeers are we,
And we're off on the daily catering spree.

Behold the maze of fragrant aisles,
The gleaming arc of clerkly smiles,
The placards daily decked with prices,
The tang of coffee, fruit and spices.
The fans with slow revolving arms
Diffuse these aromatic charms,
And titillate the multitude
That swarms about the throne of food.

Bring on your beans, bring on your peas,
And a head of garden lettuce, please;
Bring beets and carrots, bring even spinach;
Yea, onions bring; we shall not flinach.
Bring lemons, boy, and bulging grapes,
And gnarlèd squash in varying shapes;
Pile bumper crops about the ears
Of these two jolly marketeers.

Ho for the Meat Department now,
And a piece of pig or sheep or cow.
See where the glossy liver shines,
And the roast in opulence reclines,
Where every fowl upon its hook
Dreams of meeting the perfect cook,
And hamburger of the honest-to-Godest
Awaits the caterer more modest.

Mark how the scales with rapture flutter,
Weighing two pounds of cooking butter!
How buxom the bread in its paper gown —
Two loaves of white and one of brown.
How catholic the grocer's scope,

With flour and vanilla, honey and soap!
How hard for marketeers to say,
"Thank you, we think that's all today."

THE PIGEON

There is nothing in any religion
Which compels us to love the pigeon.

PIPE DREAMS

Many people have asked me what was the most beau-
    tiful sight I saw during the recent summer,
And I think the most beautiful sight was the day the
    water wouldn't stop running and in came the
    plumber,
Because your cottage may be very cunning,
But you don't appreciate it when the water won't stop
    running,
And you would almost rather submit to burgling
Than to consistent gurgling.
And then the other most beautiful sight I saw during
    the summer
Was the day the water wouldn't run at all and in came
    the plumber,
Because one thing even less enticing than a mess of
    pottage
Is a waterless cottage.

So apparently all my beautiful memories of the sum-
    mer
Are beautiful memories of the plumber,
And I am sorry they aren't more romantic,
I am sorry they are not memories of the moonlight
    rippling on the Atlantic,
Oh my yes, what wouldn't I give for some beautiful
    memories of the fields and the sky and the sea,
But they are not for the likes of me,
Nay, if you want to have beautiful memories of the
    summer,
Why the thing to do is to be a plumber,
Because then you can have some really beautiful beau-
    ties to remember,
Because naturally plumbers wouldn't think plumbers
    were the most beautiful thing they saw between
    June and September,
And that's the great advantage plumbers have over me
    and you,
They don't have to think about plumbers, so they can
    concentrate on the view.

SEASIDE SERENADE

It begins when you smell a funny smell,
And it isn't vanilla or caramel,
And it isn't forget-me-nots or lilies,
Or new-mown hay, or daffy-down-dillies,
And it's not what the barber rubs on father,
And it's awful, and yet you like it rather.
No, it's not what the barber rubs on Daddy,

It's more like an elderly finnan haddie,
Or, shall we say, an electric fan
Blowing over a sardine can.
It smells of seaweed, it smells of clams,
It's as fishy as first-night telegrams,
It's as fishy as millions of fishy fishes,
In spite of which you find it delishes,
You could do with a second helping, please,
And that, my dears, is the ocean breeze.
And pretty soon you observe a pack
Of people reclining upon their back,
And another sight that is very common
Is people reclining upon their abdomen.
And now you lose the smell of the ocean
In the sweetish vapor of sunburn lotion,
And the sun itself seems paler and colder,
Compared to vermilion face and shoulder.
Athletic young men uncover their torso
In the virile way that maidens adore so,
While paunchy uncles, before they bathe them,
In voluminous beach robes modestly swathe them.
The beach is peppered with ladies who look
Like pictures out of a medical book,
Like burlicue queens, like bubble dancers;
Their clothes are riddles complete with answers.
Last, not least, consider the kiddies,
Chirping like crickets and Katydiddies,
Splashing, squealing, slithering, crawling,
Cheerful, tearful, boisterous, bawling,
Kiddies in clamorous crowds that swarm
Heavily over your prostrate form,
Callous kiddies who gallop in myriads

'Twixt ardent Apollos and eager Nereids,
Kiddies who bring, as a priceless cup,
Something dead that a wave washed up.
Well, it's each to his taste, and a taste to each;
Shall we saunter down to the bathing beach?

ABDICATION OF A JESTER

Once there was a man and he wasn't famous for his
    clothes,
He was famous for his bon mots.
Dinner parties waited hungrily if he didn't come in
    till late
Because they could count on him to scintillate;
Just give him a cocktail or two to relax him
And you would be repaid with an epigram or a maxim;
He was invariably original,
And he did not have to depend for his effect on the
    indelicate or sacrileginal;
Of quips and anecdotes he was a warehouse,
And everybody wanted him at their house.
Yes indeed, he was quite a wit,
And then one day he suddenly quit.
He seldom went out and when he did go out he seldom
    opened his mouth,
And when he did, it was only to remark on the current
    blizzard or flood or drouth;
On scintillation he clamped down a total embargo,
And his most stimulating remark to a dinner partner in
    three months was, So you're from Louisville, I
    used to know some people named Perkins in Louis-

ville, but it seems to me I heard they'd moved to Chicago.

And at first everybody was patient but at last their brows grew darkling,

And they went to him and said, Look here, how about a little sparkling?

And he said, Do you see these lips?

And they said they did, and he said, Well they shall never more be crossed by wanton wiles and cranks and quips.

He said, I have spent my life studying the fundamentals of wit and humor and table talk,

I have spent a fortune in time and effort to master the art of stimulating and able talk;

To every aphorism of mine you ever quoted,

Why, years of experience were devoted,

And then, he said, and then the baby is told to speak to Mr. Katz the grocer on the telephone, Go ahead, baby, speak to Mr. Katz, and the baby says Meow,

And the spasms of mirth raised by baby's repartee still echo in my ears right now.

No, he said, hereafter count me not a wit, count me simply a good neighbor.

I am too old and proud to compete with unskilled labor.

LINES TO A THREE-NAME LADY

Mrs. Hattie Boomer Spink,
You puzzle me a lot.

Do you, I wonder, ever think?
And, if you do, of what?

Oh, solons bow like slender reeds
Beneath your firm resolve.
Your words I know, I know your deeds —
But whence do they evolve?

Do you employ a cerebrum,
And eke a cerebellum?
Or do you simply let 'em come,
With Gabriel at the hellum?

Nay, show me not your LL.D.
From Oklahoma Christian;
This honorary verdegree
Doth only beg the question.

Your native mental processes
Imply some secret canker;
Instead of thoughts, antipathies;
Instead of reason, rancor.

The ripple in your skull that spreads
From some primeval pebble,
How quickly washes o'er the heads
Of prophet and of rebel!

You three-name women, Mrs. Spink,
You puzzle me a lot.
Do you, I wonder, ever think?
And if you do, of what?

When gossip first began to link
Your name with that of Mr. Spink,
O Hattie Boomer, did you think?
— And what's become of Mr. Spink?

TO BARGAIN, TOBOGGAN, TO-WHOO!

There is one form of argument that though I am a
voicer of I can't see the good of,

And that is, arguing that you can afford something you
can't afford just because it doesn't cost much more
than something you also can't afford would of.

You pass up going to the movies because your finances
are in doubt,

And then you suddenly pat yourselves on the back for
passing them up and say We passed them up,
therefore we can afford to take dinner out;

And the dinner costs five dollars, but the movies would
have cost seventy cents,

So the dinner only really cost four-thirty which for the
dinner you had is not so immense,

So you go out and dance and the least you pay is ten
dollars for cover charge plus slaking your thirst,

But you still figure you have saved five or six dollars because you didn't go to the theater first,

So eventually you go to bed,

And you wake up in the morning with the glorious feeling that you are several dollars ahead,

So you start out the day being ahead by several dollars,
And then you read an advertisement saying that some-

body has removed thirty per cent from the price of
their ties and socks and collars,

So although the ties and socks and collars you already
have are still pretty clean,

Why you go in and order fifty dollars' worth because
by spending fifty dollars you can save fifteen,

So take the fifteen that you save on the ties and socks
and collars plus what you saved the night before
and it is obvious that you have saved about twenty,

Which for a twenty-four-hour thrift account strikes you
as plenty,

So then you really get the economical urge,

And then you really begin to splurge,

And you look on every splurge as a fairy godmother's
gift

Because you charge it all up to thrift,

Because the more you spend, the more you save, so you
naturally spend enormous amounts,

Because whether you can pay for it or not, it's the prin-
ciple of thrift that counts,

So it ends up with your starting out by saving the
seventy cents that you would have squandered at
your neighborhood cinema,

And really and truly ends up by your saving two hundred or two thousand, depending on whether you
have spent twenty dollars or twenty thousand to
save it, which just depends on your financial max-
ima and minima.

Roses red and jonquils gold,
I know a girl who is two years old.
Hyacinth white and violets blue,
She was very good, so now she's two.
The rabbit there on the corner shelf,
He wishes that he were two, himself,
And Little Bo Peep on the silver cup
Says, "Gracious, Linell is growing up!"
And the faithful music box simply burns
To wish her many happy returns.
The cows in the meadow murmur, "Moo!
To think that child has arrived at two!"
The cows in the meadow moo and mutter,
And send their specialest milk and butter.
The cardinal on the window sill
Greets the news with an extra trill,
The mocking bird and the dandy jay
With kindest respects salute the day,
And the swaggering crow admits his awe,
Cawing a splendid birthday caw,
And the squirrel hoists his bushy tail
In the squirrel manner of crying "Hail!"

Roses red and violets blue,
I know a girl who is really two.
Yesterday she was only one;
Today, I think, will be twice the fun.
For all good things come double fold
When a good girl gets to be two years old.
Double the number of stairs to climb,

And maybe some of them two at a time;
Double the songs and double the dances,
Double the grave and merry fancies;
Double the dolls to undress and scrub,
Double the ducks in the evening tub;
Double walks in exciting lanes,
And double trips to wave at the trains;
And certainly, double stories told
When a good girl gets to be two years old.
Linell, Linell, is it really true?
Do you faithfully promise that you are two?
Kiss me again for a lucky start
And Happy Birthday, with twice my heart!

I ALWAYS SAY A GOOD SAINT IS NO WORSE THAN A BAD COLD

Some sing of Alexander,
And some of Hercules,
And others sing of any old thing
They calculate will please.
O picayune, pallid bardlets,
Who peddle the spark divine!
Out of the way, while I fashion a lay
For good Saint Valentine.
For noble Valentine, tra-la!
For splendid Valentine!
I claim there ain't
Another Saint
As great as Valentine.

Some swear by Mother Pinkham,
And some by Father John,
While others shout for sauerkraut
To build their bodies on.
These patented panaceas
Arouse no cheers of mine —
Let us rise in force and all endorse
The good Saint Valentine.
The genial Valentine, ta-ra!
The kindly Valentine!
What can't be endured
Is quickly cured
By Doctor Valentine.

O you who woo the widow,
And you who woo the deb,
And you, and you, yes all who woo,
Give thanks for the middle of Feb.!
The coy and timorous creature
Who shrinks from your passionate line
Will leap from her cell like Ethel M. Dell
At a nod from Valentine.
From smiling Valentine, tra-la!
From virtuous Valentine!
We'd never annex
The female sex
Without Saint Valentine.

THE EGG

Let's think of eggs.
They have no legs.
Chickens come from eggs
But they have legs.
The plot thickens;
Eggs come from chickens,
But have no legs under 'em.
What a conundrum!

OH, DID YOU GET THE TICKETS? BECAUSE
I DON'T THINK I'LL GO, AFTER ALL

Women are more privileged than men, because if a
man hasn't any muscle he can't be muscular,
But even if a woman hasn't any bustle she can still be
buscular,
And women have one particular important privilege,
Which is changing their mind, which we shall call
swivelege.
Yes, the path by which they arrive at their final de-
cisions is a devious one,
And somehow they never communicate their final de-
cision to you until you have acted irrevocably on
their previous one,
Because some women may go so far as to treat some
men leniently,
But never to the extent of changing their mind help-
fully if they can change it inconveniently.
Just as it really begins to rain they announce that what

they would simply adore is gumdrops, and you
mention the rain, and they give you a look that
implies that your spine is spaghetti and your soul
is lard,

So you say you will go get the gumdrops and they
thank you sweetly and say for heaven's sake don't
get the squashy kind, get them good and hard,

So you go out and you have to go to three places before you can unearth the hard kind, and you return dripping and hand the box over and they
gaze at you with dreamy eyes as if they had just
been gazing on some angelic vision aloft,

And they say they are so sorry but right after you went
out they remembered that a fortuneteller told
them hard gumdrops were unlucky, would you
mind exchanging these for soft?

And sometimes they get you to go to an auction and
overbid extravagantly for a clock of ormolu,

And if you protest they say, " 'Oo doesn't know anysing
about art, 'oo dreat big darling subnormal 'oo,"

And an hour later they say, "That clock wasn't the right
shape for the mantelpiece, was it?"

So they ask you to calmly go back and calmly ask the
auctioneer to return your deposit.

Oh, a boy's will is the wind's will, if we are to believe
the poet,

But a girl's will is a won't, but not until it doesn't do
you any good to know it.

EDOUARD

A bugler named Dougal MacDougal
Found ingenious ways to be frugal.
He learned how to sneeze
In various keys,
Thus saving the price of a bugle.

THE SEVEN SPIRITUAL AGES OF
MRS. MARMADUKE MOORE

Mrs. Marmaduke Moore, at the age of ten
(Her name was Jemima Jevons then),
Was the quaintest of little country maids.
Her pigtails slapped on her shoulderblades;
She fed the chickens, and told the truth
And could spit like a boy through a broken tooth.
She could climb a tree to the topmost perch,
And she used to pray in the Methodist church.

At the age of twenty her heart was pure,
And she caught the fancy of Mr. Moore.
He broke his troth (to a girl named Alice),
And carried her off to his city palace,
Where she soon forgot her childhood piety
And joined in the orgies of high society.
Her voice grew English, or, say, Australian,
And she studied to be an Episcopalian.

At thirty our lives are still before us,
But Mr. Moore had a friend in the chorus.
Connubial bliss was overthrown

And Mrs. Moore now slumbered alone.
Hers was a nature that craved affection;
She gave herself up to introspection;
Then, finding theosophy rather dry,
Found peace in the sweet Bahai and Bahai.

Forty! and still an abandoned wife.
She felt old urges stirring to life.
She dipped her locks in a bowl of henna
And booked a passage through to Vienna.
She paid a professor a huge emolument
To demonstrate what his ponderous volume meant.
Returning, she preached to the unemployed
The gospel according to St. Freud.

Fifty! she haunted museums and galleries,
And pleased young men by augmenting their salaries.
Oh, it shouldn't occur, but it does occur,
That poets are made by fools like her.
Her salon was full of frangipani,
Roumanian, Russian and Hindustani,
And she conquered par as well as bogey
By reading a book and going Yogi.

Sixty! and time was on her hands —
Maybe remorse and maybe glands.
She felt a need for a free confession,
To publish each youthful indiscretion,
And before she was gathered to her mothers,
To compare her sinlets with those of others,
Mrs. Moore gave a joyous whoop,
And immersed herself in the Oxford group.

That is the story of Mrs. Moore,
As far as it goes. But of this I'm sure —
When seventy stares her in the face
She'll have found some other state of grace.
Mohammed may be her Lord and master,
Or Zeus, or Mithros or Zoroaster.
For when a lady is badly sexed
God knows what God is coming next.

THE STRANGE CASE OF THE AMBITIOUS CADDY

Once upon a time there was a boy named Robin Bide-
awee.

∽

He had chronic hiccups.

∽

He had hay fever, too.

∽

Also, he was learning to whistle through his teeth.

∽

Oh yes, and his shoes squeaked.

∽

The scoutmaster told him he had better be a caddy.

∽

He said, Robin, you aren't cut out for a scout, you're
cut out for a caddy.

∽

At the end of Robin's first day as a caddy the caddymaster asked him how he got along.

∽

Robin said, I got along fine but my man lost six balls, am I ready yet?

∽

The caddymaster said No, he wasn't ready yet.

∽

At the end of the second day the caddymaster asked him again how he got along.

∽

Robin said, My man left me behind to look for a ball on the fourth hole and I didn't catch up to him till the eighteenth, am I ready yet?

∽

The caddymaster said No, he wasn't ready yet.

∽

Next day Robin said, I only remembered twice to take the flag on the greens and when I did take it I wiggled it, am I ready yet?

∽

The caddymaster said No, he wasn't ready yet.

∽

Next day Robin said, My man asked me whether he had a seven or an eight on the water hole and I said an eight, am I ready yet?

∽

The caddymaster said No, he wasn't ready yet.

∽

Next day Robin said, Every time my man's ball stopped on the edge of a bunker I kicked it in, am I ready yet?

∽

The caddymaster said No, he wasn't ready yet.

∽

Next day Robin said, I never once handed my man the club he asked for, am I ready yet?

∞

The caddymaster said No, he wasn't ready yet.

∞

Next day Robin said, I bet a quarter my man would lose and told him so, am I ready yet?

∞

The caddymaster said, Not quite.

∞

Next day Robin said, I laughed at my man all the way round, am I ready yet?

∞

The caddymaster said, Have you still got hiccups, and have you still got hay fever, and are you still learning how to whistle through your teeth, and do your shoes still squeak?

∞

Robin said, Yes, yes, a thousand times yes.

∞

Then you are indeed ready, said the caddymaster.

∞

Tomorrow you shall caddy for Ogden Nash.

AFTER THE CHRISTENING

Come along, everybody, see the pretty baby,
Such a pretty baby ought to be adored.
Come along, everybody, come and bore the baby,
See the pretty baby, begging to be bored.

Hurry, hurry, Aunt Louise,
Silly names are sure to please.
Bother what the baby thinks!
Call her Kitchy-kitch and Binks,
Call her Wackywoo and Snookums,
Just ignore her dirty lookums,
Who than she is fairer game
For every kind of silly name?
Baby cannot answer back,
Or perhaps an aunt she'd lack.

Come along, everybody, isn't she a darling?
Such a little darling ought to be enjoyed.
Come along, everybody, let's annoy the baby,
Such a darling darling begs to be annoyed.

Goodness Gracious, Uncle George!
Home at last from Valley Forge?
Won't you try on her the whoops
That cheered the Continental troops?
Stand a little closer, please;
That will put her at her ease;
And babies find it hard to hear,
So place your mouth against her ear —
I guess she heard it, Uncle George;
I'm sure they did at Valley Forge.

Come along, everybody, see the little lady,
Isn't she adorable and kissable and pleasing?
Come along, everybody, come and tease the baby,
Here's a lady baby available for teasing!

Cousin Charles was always chummy;
He's about to poke her tummy.
Grandpa almost chokes on chuckles,
Tickling with his beard her knuckles;
All of Granny's muscles ache
From half an hour of patty-cake;
God-mamma with glee begins
A noisy count of baby's chins;
God-papa with humor glows
Playing piggie with her toes.
See the happy prideful parents,
Do they think of interference?
Certainly not, while baby gives
Such wholesome fun to relatives.

Up and at her, everybody, at the pretty baby,
Tell her she's a dumpling, tell her she's a dear.
Everybody knows the way to woo a baby —
Tickle her and pinch her and yodel in her ear.

THE GERM

A mighty creature is the germ,
Though smaller than the pachyderm.
His customary dwelling place
Is deep within the human race.
His childish pride he often pleases
By giving people strange diseases.
Do you, my poppet, feel infirm?
You probably contain a germ.

Lots of truisms don't have to be repeated but there is one
    that has got to be,

Which is that it is much nicer to be happy than it is not
    to be,

And I shall even add to it by stating unequivocally and
    without restraint

That you are much happier when you are happy than
    when you ain't.

Some people are just naturally Pollyanna,

While others call for sugar and cream and strawberries
    on their manna.

Now, I think we all ought to say a fig for the happiness
    that comes of thinking helpful thoughts and search-
    ing your soul,

The most exciting happiness is the happiness generated
    by forces beyond your control,

Because if you just depend on your helpful thoughts for
    your happiness and would just as soon drink butter-
    milk as champagne, and if mink is no better than
    lapin to you,

Why you don't even deserve to have anything nice and
    exciting happen to you.

If you are really Master of your Fate,

It shouldn't make any difference to you whether Cleo-
    patra or the Bearded Lady is your mate,

So I hold no brief for the kind of happiness or the kind
    of unhappiness that some people constantly carry
    around in their breast,

Because that kind of happiness simply consists of being

resigned to the worst just as that kind of unhappi-
ness consists of being resentful of the best.

No, there is only one kind of happiness that I take the
stump for,

Which is the kind that comes when something so wonderful falls in your lap that joy is what you jump for,

Something not of your own doing,

When the blue sky opens and out pops a refund from
the Government or an invitation to a terrapin dinner
or an unhoped-for Yes from the lovely creature you
have been disconsolately wooing.

And obviously such miracles don't happen every day,

But here's hoping they may,

Because then everybody would be happy except the
people who pride themselves on creating their own
happiness who as soon as they saw everybody who
didn't create their own happiness happy they would
probably grieve over sharing their own heretofore
private sublimity,

A condition which I could face with equanimity.

PRIDE GOETH BEFORE A RAISE,
or
AH, THERE, MRS. CADWALLADER–SMITH!

The Cadwallader-Smiths
Are People with Poise;
I consider them one of the minor joys,
Though frequently wishing
That I could share
Their imperturbable savoir-faire.

Madame is a modishly youthful matron,
Artfully dyed and I think enameled;
Monsieur is a generous opera patron,
A Man-about-Town, by trade untrammeled.
Oh the dapper dandies,
The haughty dames,
In the phalanx of hy-
Phenated names!
(Have you ever observed
That the name of Smith
Is the oftenest hy-
Phenated with?)
In the days when they acted namby-pambily
Madame and Monsieur acquired a fambily,
Which accounts for the junior Cadwallader-Smiths,
Those perennial rotogravurian myths,
Maidens who scale the Alps and Rockies,
Debutantes with the world in tow,
Polo players and gentleman jockeys,
And athletes tailored in Savile Row.
Oh glamorous girls and golden boys,
They practically palpitate with poise!
Say me a word. It's a word they've got.
So what?

Well, though hardly copy for a great biographer,
They know how to twinkle for a news photographer.
They don't go to work, but they wallow in shekels,
And they sit on beaches and don't get freckles.
They exchange divorces without bearing malice,
And they all get presented at Buckingham Palace.
They receive reporters with a nonchalant air,

And they're dignified even in the barber chair,
They are dignified even in their testimonials
To beautifying lotions for the crude Colonials.
They take a paper and they read the headlines,
So they've heard of unemployment and they've heard of
    breadlines,
And they philanthropically cure them all
By getting up a costume charity ball.
They own a mansion in the borough of Manhattan
Which they use about as much as Greek and Latin,
And they tipple nectar and they nibble lotus,
And they pay no attention to a jury notus,
And they don't get a summons when they run past stop-
    lights,
So they have the point of view of true cosmopolites,
And they look you in the eye through their gold lor-
    gnettes
And advise cancellation of the foreign debts.
They could all pay taxes, but they'd rather not.
So what?

Well, they're People with Poise,
The Cadwallader-Smiths,
With the sensitive senses of monoliths,
Which I freely admit
I could use myself,
Had I all I desire of profit and pelf.

A WORD ON WIND

Cows go around saying Moo,

But the wind goes around saying Woooo.

Ghosts say Woooo to you, too,

And sometimes they say Boo to you, too,

But everybody has heard the wind and few people have
heard a ghost,

So it is commonly supposed that the wind says Woooo
the most.

Scientists try to tell us that wind is caused by atmospheric
conditions at the North Pole or over distant Cana-
dian ranches,

But I guess scientists don't ever get to the country, because everybody who has ever been in the country
knows that wind is caused by the trees waggling
their branches.

On the ocean, where there are no trees, they refer to
the wind as "gales,"

And it is probably caused by whales,

And in the Sahara, where there are no trees or whales,
either, they call the wind a simoom or something,

And it is the result of the profanation of Tutankhamen's
tomb or something.

Ill winds blow nobody good and they also blow new hats
into mud puddles and voracious clouds of mosquitoes into propinquity with your hide,

And they make your cigarette burn down on just one
side.

Some people are very refined,

And when they recite poetry or sing songs they pro-
nounce wind "wined,"

Well dear Wined, every time you say Wooooo,
Why I wish you would say it to people who say "wined,"
    right after you have said it somewhere where some-
    body is making fertilizer or glue.

THE WOMBAT

The wombat lives across the seas,
Among the far Antipodes.
He may exist on nuts and berries,
Or then again, on missionaries;
His distant habitat precludes
Conclusive knowledge of his moods.
But I would not engage the wombat
In any form of mortal combat.

COLUMBUS

Once upon a time there was an Italian,
And some people thought he was a rapscallion,
But he wasn't offended,
Because other people thought he was splendid,
And he said the world was round,
And everybody made an uncomplimentary sound,
But he went and tried to borrow some money from
    Ferdinand
But Ferdinand said America was a bird in the bush and
    he'd rather have a berdinand,
But Columbus' brain was fertile, it wasn't arid,

And he remembered that Ferdinand was married,

And he thought, there is no wife like a misunderstood
one,

Because if her husband thinks something is a terrible
idea she is bound to think it a good one,

So he perfumed his handkerchief with bay rum and
citronella,

And he went to see Isabella,

And he looked wonderful but he had never felt sillier,

And she said, I can't place the face but the aroma is
familiar,

And Columbus didn't say a word,

All he said was, I am Columbus, the fifteenth-century
Admiral Byrd,

And, just as he thought, her disposition was very mallea-
ble,

And she said, Here are my jewels, and she wasn't penuri-
ous like Cornelia the mother of the Gracchi, she
wasn't referring to her children, no, she was referring
to her jewels, which were very very valuable,

So Columbus said, Somebody show me the sunset and
somebody did and he set sail for it,

And he discovered America and they put him in jail
for it,

And the fetters gave him welts,

And they named America after somebody else,

So the sad fate of Columbus ought to be pointed out to
every child and every voter,

Because it has a very important moral, which is, Don't
be a discoverer, be a promoter.

THE COW

The cow is of the bovine ilk;
One end is moo, the other, milk.

SONG FOR A TEMPERATURE OF A HUNDRED AND ONE

Of all God's creatures give me man
For impractical uniqueness,
He's hardly tenth when it comes to strenth,
But he leads the field in weakness.
Distemper suits the ailing dog,
The chicken's content with pip,
But the human race, which sets the pace,
Takes nothing less than Grippe.

THEN, hey for the grippe, for the goodly la grippe!
In dogs it's distemper, in chickens it's pip;
But the lords of creation insist at the least
On the germ that distinguishes man from the beast.

The mule with mange is satisfied,
Or hookworm in the South;
And the best-bred kine consider it fine
To toy with hoof-and-mouth;
Bubonic cheers the humble rat
As he happily leaves the ship;
When the horse gets botts he thinks it's lots,
But people hold out for grippe.

THEN, hey for the grippe, for the goodly la grippe,
For the frog in the throat and the chap on the lip;
For the ice on the feet and the fire on the brow,
And the bronchial tubes that moo like a cow.
And hey for the ache in the back of the legs,
And the diet of consommé, water and eggs,
For the mustard that sits on your chest like a cactus,
For the doctor you're kindly providing with practus;
And hey for the pants of which you're so fond,
And the first happy day they're allowed to be donned;
For the first day at work, all bundled in wraps,
And last but not least, for the splendid relapse.
So let man meet his Maker, a smile on his lip,
Singing hey, double hey, for the goodly la grippe.

SOME OF MY BEST FRIENDS ARE CHILDREN

Ichneumons are fond of little ichneumons,
And lions of little lions,
But I am not fond of little humans;
I do not believe in scions.

Of course there's always our child,
But our child is different,
Our child appeals
To the cultivated mind.
Ours is a lady;
Boys are odoriferant;
Ladies are the sweetness;
Boys are the rind.

Whenever whimsy collides with whimsy
As parents compare their cherubs,
At the slightest excuse, however flimsy,
I fold my tent like the Arubs.

Of course there's always our child,
But our child is charminger,
Our child's eyes
Are a special kind of blue;
Our child's smile
Is quite a lot disarminger;
Our child's tooth
Is very nearly through.

Mankind, I consider, attained its zenith
The day it achieved the adult;
When the conversation to infants leaneth,
My horse is bridled and saddult.

Of course there's always our child,
But our child is wittier;
Our child's noises
Are the nicest kind of noise;
She has no beard
Like Tennyson or Whittier;
But Tennyson and Whittier
Began as little boys.

The Politician, the Parent, the Preacher,
Were each of them once a kiddie.
The child is indeed a talented creature.
Do I want one? Oh God forbidde!

Of course there's always our child
But our child's adorable.
Our child's an angel
Fairer than the flowers;
Our child fascinates
One who's rather borable;
And incidentally,
Our child is ours.

JANGLE BELLS

Snow is all right while it is snowing;
It is like inebriation, because it is very pleasing when it
    is coming, but very unpleasing when it is going,
But any further resemblance between the two has
    escaped this Old Master,
Because certainly everybody would rather be sozzled
    than snowbound, except maybe Mrs. Ella Boole and
    Lady Astor.

NATURE KNOWS BEST

People have been getting up for centuries,
They have been getting up in palaces and Pullmans and
    penitentiaries.
Yes, one fact for which every historian vouches,
Is that every morning in history began with people get-
    ting up off their couches.
The caveman had to get up before he could go out and
    track the brontosaurus,

Verdi had to get up before he could sit down and compose the Anvil Chorus,

Alexander had to get up before he could go around being
dominant,

Even Rip Van Winkle had to get up from one sleep before he could climb the mountain and encounter
the sleep which has made him prominent.

Some get up energetically and some in lassitude's throes,

And I myself happen to love a lassitude, a bonnie bonnie
lassitude, but be that as it may, however they rose,
they rose.

Well, birds are descended from birds and flowers are
descended from flowers,

And human beings are descended from generation after
generation of ancestors who got up at least once
every twenty-four hours,

And since birds are descended from birds they don't have
to be forced to sing like birds, instead of squeaking
like rats,

And since flowers are descended from flowers they don't
have to be forced to smell like flowers, instead of
like burning rubber or the Jersey flats,

But you take human beings, why their countless genera-
tions of ancestors who were always arising might just
as well have spent all their lives on their mattresses
or pallets,

Because their descendants haven't inherited any talent
for getting up at all, no, every morning they have to
be forced to get up either by their own conscience
or somebody else's, or alarm clocks or valets.

Well, there is one obvious conclusion that I have always
held to,

Which is that if Nature had really intended human beings to get up, why they would get up naturally and
wouldn't have to be compelled to.

A PARABLE FOR SPORTS WRITERS, SOCIETY
COLUMNISTS, BOND SALESMEN AND POETS,
or
GO GET A REPUTATION

I

Ezra Æsop, at eighty-eight,
He published a volume of verse.
The rhymes were ragged,
The meter wilted,
The prosody prosy,
The stanzas stilted.
But other poets of eighty-eight,
Patriarchal or celibate,
Might — conceivably —
Might — believably —
Might — finally, irretrievably —
Have seized the muse by the horns and tail,
And written a volume worse.
So the red fires burned,
And the banners flew,
And the fat nymphs danced
In the pagan dew,
And the mountains skipped like little lambs,
And editors squandered telegrams,
And over deserts,
And under oceans,

Through Rotary, Red Men, Elks and Yosians,
The word flew East and the word flew West,
Flew with the wings of a drummer's jest,
That the book of the era, beyond debate,
Was the book by the poet of eighty-eight.
O, Excellent Ezra! the people cried,
He might have doddered,
He might have died,
He might have entered a monastery,
He might have adopted his secretary.
But what did he do?
He studied at home,
Then up and published a slender tome.
So they borrowed early and purchased late
The book by the poet of eighty-eight,
And El Dorado had no bonanzas
Like Ezra Æsop's elderly stanzas.

II

Rosalie Ransome, going on six,
She published a volume, too,
And Heaven pity the heretics
Who neglected to read it through.
For the word was out,
In palace and cot,
Of the teensy, weensy, talented tot,
And gangsters gossiped of Rosalie Ransome,
Who lisped iambics,
And lisped 'em handsome.
The public panted,
The press grew giddy,

At the very thought
Of a lyrical kiddy,
And professors pawned their Shelley and Keats
To purchase Rosalie's youthful feats.

III

A regular poet published a book,
And an excellent book it was,
But nobody gave it a second look,
As nobody often does.
He was going on half-past thirty-five,
So it didn't keep him long alive.

ENGLAND EXPECTS—

Let us pause to consider the English,
Who when they pause to consider themselves they get
    all reticently thrilled and tinglish,
Because every Englishman is convinced of one thing,
    viz.:
That to be an Englishman is to belong to the most ex-
    clusive club there is;
A club to which benighted bounders of Frenchmen and
    Germans and Italians et cetera cannot even aspire to
    belong,
Because they don't even speak English, and the Ameri-
    cans are worst of all because they speak it wrong.
Englishmen are distinguished by their traditions and
    ceremonials,

And also by their affection for their Colonies and their
    contempt for their Colonials.

When foreigners ponder world affairs, why sometimes by
    doubt they are smitten,

But Englishmen know instinctively that what the world
    needs most is whatever is best for Great Britain.

They have a splendid Navy and they conscientiously ad-
    mire it,

And every English schoolboy knows that John Paul Jones
    was only an unfair American pirate.

English people disclaim sparkle and verve,

But speak without reservations of their Anglo-Saxon re-
    serve.

After listening to little groups of English ladies and
    gentlemen at cocktail parties and in hotels and Pull-
    mans, of defining Anglo-Saxon reserve I despair

But I think it consists of assuming that nobody else is
    there,

And I shudder to think where Anglo-Saxon reserve ends
    when I consider where it begins,

Which is in a few high-pitched statements of what one's
    income is and just what foods give one a rash and
    whether one and one's husband or wife sleep in a
    double bed or twins.

All good young Englishmen go to Oxford or Cambridge
    and they all write and publish books before their
    graduation,

And I often wondered how they did it until I realized
    that they have to do it because their genteel accents
    are so developed that they can no longer understand
    each other's spoken words, so the written word is
    their only means of intercommunication.

England is the last home of the aristocracy, and the art
of protecting the aristocracy from the encroach-
ments of commerce has been raised to quite an art,
Because in America a rich butter-and-egg man is only a
rich butter-and-egg man or at most an honorary
LL.D. of some hungry university, but in England
why before he knows it he is Sir Benjamin Buttery,
Bart.
Anyhow, I think the English people are sweet,
And we might as well get used to them because when
they slip and fall they always land on their own or
somebody else's feet.

AWAY FROM IT ALL

I wish I were a Tibetan monk
Living in a monastery.
I would unpack my trunk
And store it in a tronastery;
I would collect all my junk
And send it to a jonastery;
I would try to reform a drunk,
And pay his expenses at a dronastery.
And if my income shrunk
I would send it to a shronastery.

LOOK WHAT YOU DID, CHRISTOPHER!

In fourteen hundred and ninety-two,
Somebody sailed the ocean blue.

Somebody borrowed the fare in Spain
For a business trip on the bounding main,
And to prove to people, by actual test,
You could get to the East by traveling West.
Somebody said, Sail on! Sail on!
And studied China and China's lingo,
And cried from the bow, There's China now!
And promptly bumped into San Domingo.
Somebody murmured, Oh dear, oh dear!
I've discovered the Western Hemisphere.

And that, you may think, my friends, was that.
But it wasn't. Not by a fireman's hat.
Well enough wasn't left alone,
And Columbus was only a cornerstone.
There came the Spaniards,
There came the Greeks,
There came the Pilgrims in leather breeks.
There came the Dutch,
And the Poles and Swedes,
The Persians, too,
And perhaps the Medes,
The Letts the Laps and the Lithuanians,
Regal Russians, and ripe Roumanians.
There came the French
And there came the Finns,
And the Japanese
With their friendly grins.
The Tartars came,
And the Terrible Turks —
In a word, humanity shot the works.
And the country that should have been Cathay

Decided to be
The U.S.A.

And that, you may think, my friends, was that.
But it wasn't. Not by a fireman's hat.
Christopher C. was the cornerstone,
And well enough wasn't left alone.
For those who followed
When he was through,
They burned to discover something, too.
Somebody, bored with rural scenery,
Went to work and invented machinery,
While a couple of other mental giants
Got together
And thought up Science.
Platinum blondes
(They were once peroxide),
Peruvian bonds
And carbon monoxide,
Tax evaders
And Vitamin A,
Vice crusaders,
And tattle-tale gray —
These, with many another phobia,
We owe to that famous Twelfth of Octobia.
O misery, misery, mumble and moan!
Someone invented the telephone,
And interrupted a nation's slumbers,
Ringing wrong but similar numbers.
Someone devised the silver screen
And the intimate Hollywood magazine,
And life is a Hades

Of clicking cameras,
And foreign ladies
Behaving amorous.
Gags have erased
Amusing dialog,
As gas replaced
The crackling firelog.
All that glitters is sold as gold,
And our daily diet grows odder and odder,
And breakfast foods are dusty and cold —
It's a wise child
That knows its fodder.
Someone invented the automobile,
And good Americans took the wheel
To view American rivers and rills
And justly famous forests and hills —
But somebody equally enterprising
Had invented billboard advertising.
You linger at home
In dark despair,
And wistfully try the electric air.
You hope against hope for a quizz imperial,
And what do they give you?
A doctor serial.
Oh, Columbus was only a cornerstone,
And well enough wasn't left alone,
For the Inquisition was less tyrannical
Than the iron rules of an age mechanical,
Which, because of an error in '92,
Are clamped like corsets on me and you,
While Children of Nature we'd be today
If San Domingo
Had been Cathay.

And that, you may think, my friends, is that.
But it isn't — not by a fireman's hat.
The American people,
With grins jocose,
Always survive the fatal dose.
And though our systems are slightly wobbly,
We'll fool the doctor this time, probly.

EPILOGUE TO MOTHER'S DAY

M is for the preliminary million-dollar advertising appropriation,

O means that she is always white-haired, bespectacled and at least eighty-five years old,

T is for Telegraph message number 31B which contains a tastefully blended expression of sentiment and congratulation,

H is for the coast-to-coast questionnaire which proved conclusively that seven-and-one-half citizens out of every ten with incomes of $5000 a year or better would rather have their mother than gold.

E is for the Elephants which everybody is very glad didn't sit down on their mothers,

R is for Rosemary which is for Remembrance of the fact that a mother is one thing that you will never have more than one of,

Put them all together and before you can say H. St.C. Wellington Carruthers, they spell the second of two things that everybody who loves their mother only once a year and then only at the instigation of the Chamber of Commerce is a son of.

THE ANT

The ant has made himself illustrious
Through constant industry industrious.
So what?
Would you be calm and placid
If you were full of formic acid?

DON'T CRY, DARLING, IT'S BLOOD ALL RIGHT

Whenever poets want to give you the idea that something is particularly meek and mild,
They compare it to a child,
Thereby proving that though poets with poetry may be rife
They don't know the facts of life.
If of compassion you desire either a tittle or a jot,
Don't try to get it from a tot.
Hard-boiled, sophisticated adults like me and you
May enjoy ourselves thoroughly with Little Women and Winnie-the-Pooh,
But innocent infants these titles from their reading course eliminate
As soon as they discover that it was honey and nuts and mashed potatoes instead of human flesh that Winnie-the-Pooh and Little Women ate.
Innocent infants have no use for fables about rabbits or donkeys or tortoises or porpoises,
What they want is something with plenty of well-mutilated corpoises.

Not on legends of how the rose came to be a rose instead
   of a petunia is their fancy fed,
But on the inside story of how somebody's bones got
   ground up to make somebody else's bread.
They'll go to sleep listening to the story of the little
   beggarmaid who got to be queen by being kind to
   the bees and the birds,
But they're all eyes and ears the minute they suspect a
   wolf or a giant is going to tear some poor woodcutter
   into quarters or thirds.
It really doesn't take much to fill their cup;
All they want is for somebody to be eaten up.
Therefore I say unto you, all you poets who are so crazy
   about meek and mild little children and their angelic
   air,
If you are sincere and really want to please them, why
   just go out and get yourselves devoured by a bear.

THE PURIST

I give you now Professor Twist,
A conscientious scientist.
Trustees exclaimed, "He never bungles!"
And sent him off to distant jungles.
Camped on a tropic riverside,
One day he missed his loving bride.
She had, the guide informed him later,
Been eaten by an alligator.
Professor Twist could not but smile.
"You mean," he said, "a crocodile."

· 225 ·

THE STRANGE CASE OF THE SOCIETY
GIRL'S NECK

Once upon a time there was a girl named Thomasina Van
Thomas.

જ

She was an unfortunate girl.

જ

I do not mean in the sociological sense.

જ

She was unfortunate because she spent the greater part
of her days in tantrums.

જ

She should have been supremely happy, for she was every
inch a society girl.

જ

Her father had been investigated five times by the Senate,
and she had often been photographed among her
cigarettes.

જ

She was rich and beautiful and an adept at persiflage.

જ

But I regret to say that any fishwife could have taught
her much about self-control.

જ

She once roped the butler with her diamond necklace
and bulldogged and branded him in eleven seconds.

જ

She was angry because her caviar contained no double-
yolked eggs.

જ

Thomasina's tantrums alienated the élite of Newport, Bar Harbor, Palm Beach, Leavenworth, and the Athens water-front.

ᕤᕚᕧ

The last I heard of her, her only admirers were five florists and a dog.

ᕤᕚᕧ

The dog's name was Brother, after a sister of his mother's who had been expelled from the Bide-a-Wee Home for violation of the honor system.

ᕤᕚᕧ

The florists' names were Nicodemus.

ᕤᕚᕧ

One day they called and found her pelting a landscape architect with pigeon's-blood rubies.

ᕤᕚᕧ

It seems that she had ordered a lagoon and he had installed a mongoose.

ᕤᕚᕧ

Her admirers were alarmed by her kicks and screams, which were far from cultured.

ᕤᕚᕧ

They left her posthaste.

ᕤᕚᕧ

I think they went to call on a fishwife.

ᕤᕚᕧ

I forgot to say that a bevy of butterflies accompanied the florists on their arrival.

ᕤᕚᕧ

They didn't want to see the society girl, but they liked the florists' bouquets.

ᕤᕚᕧ

When the florists took their bouquets away the butterflies were disgusted.

ᴖ

They were so disgusted that they turned right back into
caterpillars.

ᴖ

And crawled.
Down.
The society girl's.
NECK!
Don't have tantrums.

LUCY LAKE

Lawsamassy, for heaven's sake!
Have you never heard of Lucy Lake?
Lucy is fluffy and fair and cosy,
Lucy is like a budding posy.
Lucy speaks with a tiny lisp,
Lucy's mind is a will-o'-the-wisp.
Lucy is just as meek as a mouse,
Lucy lives in a darling house,
With a darling garden and darling fence,
And a darling faith in the future tense.
A load of hay, or a crescent moon,
And she knows that things will be better soon.
Lucy resigns herself to sorrow
In building character for tomorrow.
Lucy tells us to carry on,
It's always darkest before the dawn.
A visit to Lucy's bucks you up,

Helps you swallow the bitterest cup.
Lucy Lake is meek as a mouse.
Let's go over to Lucy's house,
And let's lynch Lucy!

THE EIGHT O'CLOCK PERIL

Breakfast is a thoroughly inedible repast,
And the dictionary says it is derived from the words
break, meaning to break, and fast, meaning a fast, so
to breakfast means to break your fast.
Which definition the veriest child could see doesn't
check,
Because if the first syllable of breakfast means to break,
why is it pronounced brek?
Shame on you, you old lexicographers, I shall call you
laxicographers because you have grown very lax,
Because it is perfectly obvious that the first syllable in
breakfast is derived from the far-famed Yale football cheer, which is Brekeke-kex, Ko-ax, Ko-ax,
And did you even get the second syllable right? Why a
thousand times No,
Because the fast in breakfast doesn't mean fast, absti-
nence from food, it means fast, not slow.
So with that in mind we can peek behind the scenes
And then we can see what break-fast really means;
It means that if you wake up in the morning feeling un-
appetized and sickly,
Why you are confronted by a meal and the entire Yale
football team coaxes you with an ax to eat it quickly.
On this topic I could write a chapter,

But I will content myself with saying that the French
     word for breakfast, which is déjeuner, is considera-
     bly apter,
Because it is perfectly truthful,
Because it is made up of the words de, meaning to un-
     something, and jeuner, which must be derived from
     the word jeune, meaning young, so jeuner must
     mean to grow youthful,
So I think that is the reason that the French are always
     bright and gay,
Because they never eat breakfast because they are warned
     off it by their word for it, which means something
     that if you eat it you will grow unyouthful right
     away.

IN WHICH THE POET IS ASHAMED
BUT PLEASED

Of all the things that I would rather,
It is to be my daughter's father,
While she, with innocence divine,
Is quite contented to be mine.

I am distressingly aware
That this arrangement is unfair,
For I, when in my celibate garrison,
Acquired some standard of comparison.

I visited nurseries galore,
Compiled statistics by the score,

And gained experience from a crew
Of children passing in review.

And some were fair and some were dark
And some were clothed and some were stark,
And some were howling, teasing demons,
And some as sweet as Mrs. Hemans.

I saw the best that parents vaunted;
They weren't exactly what I wanted;
Yet, all the offspring that I faced,
They served to cultivate my taste.

Thus, let the miser praise the mintage,
And let the vintner praise the vintage;
I'm conscious that in praising her,
I'm speaking as a connoisseur.

While she, poor dear, has never known
A father other than her own.
She wots of other girls' papas
No more than of the Persian Shah's.

Within her head no notion stirs
That some are better men than hers;
That some are richer, some are kinder,
Some are solider, some refineder,

That some are vastly more amusing
Some fitter subjects for enthusing,
That some are cleverer, some are braver,
Than the one that fortune gave her.

What fortune set us side by side,
Her scope so narrow, mine so wide?
We owe to this sweet dispensation
Our mutual appreciation.

SPLASH!

Some people are do-it-some-other-timers and other peo-
    ple are do-it-nowers,
And that is why manufacturers keep on manufacturing
    both bathtubs and showers,
Because some bathers prefer to recline
On the cornerstone of their spine,
While others, who about their comfort are less particular,
Bathe perpendicular.
Thus from the way people lave themselves
You can tell how under other circumstances they will
    behave themselves.
Tubbers indulge in self-indulgence,
And they loll soaking until they are a moist mass of
    warm rosy effulgence,
And finally they regretfully hoist themselves up and
    shiver and say Brrr! even though the atmosphere is
    like an orchid-house and the mirror is coated with
    steam,
And they pat at their moistness with a towel as soft as
    whipped cream,
So it is obvious that the tubber is a sybaritic softie,
And will never accomplish anything lofty.
How different is the showerer, whose chest is often fes-

tooned with hair such as bedecked our ancestors
    arboreal!

He has no time to waste on luxuriousness, but skims
    through the spray with the speed of a Democratic
    politician skimming through a Republican editorial,

After which he grates himself on something which he
    calls a towel,

But which anybody covered with human skin instead of
    cowhide would call a file or a spur or a rowel,

So we see that the showerer is a Spartan,

And sternly guides his ambitious life along the lines laid
    down by baccalaureate preachers and Bruce Barton,

And this is the reason that in the game of life although
    occasional points are won by the tubber,

The showerer always gets game and rubber.

Sometimes tubbers and showerers get into arguments
    about tubs and showers and become very warlike
    and martial,

But I myself have always been strictly impartial,

Yes, I am neutrally anchored halfway between Calais and
    Dover,

And all I will impartially and neutrally say is that there
    are three things you can't do in a shower, and one
    is read, and the other is smoke, and the other is get
    wet all over.

THE JAPANESE

How courteous is the Japanese;
He always says, "Excuse it, please."

He climbs into his neighbor's garden,
And smiles, and says, "I beg your pardon";
He bows and grins a friendly grin,
And calls his hungry family in;
He grins, and bows a friendly bow;
"So sorry, this my garden now."

JUDGMENT DAY

This is the day, this is the day!
I knew as soon as the sun's first ray
Crept through the slats of the cot,
And opened the eyes of a tot,
And the tot would rather have slept,
And, therefore, wept.
This is the day that is wrong,
The day when the only song
Is a skirling lamentation
Of continuous indignation,
When the visage is ireful,
The voice, direful,
And the early, pearly teeth
Snick like a sword in the sheath,
When the fists are clenched,
And the cheeks are drenched
In full-fed freshets and tumbling, tumultuous torrents
Of virtuous abhorrence,
When loud as the challenging trumpets of John at Le-
        panto
Rings the clarion, "I don't want to."
This is the day, the season,

Of wrongs without reason,
The day when the prunes and the cereal
Taste like building material,
When the spinach tastes only like spinach, and honey
and sugar
Raise howls like the yells of a quarrelsome puma or
cougar,
When the wail is not to be hushed
Nor the hair to be brushed,
When life is frustration, and either
A person must be all alone or have somebody with her,
and tolerates neither,
When outdoors is worse than in, and indoors than out,
and both too dull to be borne,
And dolls are flung under the bed and books are torn,
When people humiliate a person
With their clumsily tactful attempts to conciliate a per-
son,
When music no charm possesses,
Nor hats, nor mittens, nor dresses,
When the frowning fortress is woe
And the watchword is No.
You owners of children who pass this day with forbear-
ance,
You indeed are parents!

THE UNSELFISH HUSBAND

Once upon a time there was a man named Orlando Tregennis and he was in love with his wife,
And he thought he would express his love by serenading

her but his serenade wasn't very successful because his playing interfered with his singing because all he could play was the fife,

So then he said, I will climb the highest mountain in the world and name it after my wife and then she will give me a look of love, so he climbed the highest mountain in the world and his wife was indeed whom he named it after,

But she didn't give him a look of love, she gave him a look of laughter,

And not only a look of laughter but a look of menace,

Because he named it after his wife by naming it Mt. Mrs. Orlando Tregennis,

So then he said that he certainly was sorry that during the great war he had absent-mindedly forgotten to join the Army,

Because he said if he had been entitled to a bonus he would have given her every penny even though she was already so entrancing that no amount of mere money could make her a jot or a tittle more allury or charmy,

And she greeted this remark with ribald merriment,

And she said that possibly money wouldn't get her any further than she was, but she'd like a chance to try the experiment,

So then Mr. Tregennis said, Well, I haven't any gold,

But I will give you my most precious possession, I will give you my cold,

And he gave her his cold and first of all she tried to spurn it,

And then she tried to return it,

But he said No darling, now it's your very own cold,

It is yours to have and to hold,

Because if you reckon I don't give gifts for keeps you
made a mistake when you reckoned,

Because there hasn't been an Indian-giver in the Tregennis family since my great-great-grandfather, old
Hiawatha Tregennis II.

But she wouldn't take No for an answer, but he wouldn't
say Yes, and Mr. Tregennis's precious cold went
shuttling back and forth between them for the rest
of their lives,

And I hope everybody will turn out to be such self-
sacrificing husbands and wives.

COMMON SENSE

Why did the Lord give us agility
If not to evade responsibility?

JUST A PIECE OF LETTUCE AND SOME LEMON JUICE, THANK YOU

The human body is composed
Of head and limbs and torso,
Kept slim by gents
At great expense,
By ladies, even more so.

The human waistline will succumb
To such and such a diet.

The ladies gnaw
On carrots raw,
Their husbands will not try it.

The human bulk can be compressed
By intricate devices,
Which ladies hie
In droves to buy
At pre-depression prices.

The human shape can be subdued
By rolling on the floor.
Though many wives
Thus spend their lives,
To husbands it's a bore.

Though human flesh can be controlled,
We're told, by this and that,
You cannot win:
The thin stay thin,
The fat continue fat.

MIRIAM'S LUCKY DAY

Once there was a girl named Miriam,
And she spent part of her time in a delirium,
And she said, I wish the world were a little less mys-
        terious,
Because I do like to know when I am delirious,
But I have discovered that whenever I regard the world

and judge it logical and normal and headed for the millennium at a mile a minute,

Why that's the time I ought to be enclosed in a spacious park with an asylum in it,

But whenever everybody else seems to be running around in a delirium,

Why that's the time when somebody may be fuzzy-minded, but it isn't Miriam.

So finally she convened an enormous convention, national and international,

And she said, Please I wish everybody would help me to determine when I am delirious and when I am rational,

Because, she said, at present I am just a bit hazy,

Because when I am crazy you all seem perfectly sane, but when I am sane you all seem perfectly crazy,

So, she said, forgive me if I am too personal or informal,

But I hope from now on you will all behave so that I will think you are delirious if I am delirious, and normal if I am normal,

So they all said, What a good idea, hurrah for Miriam!

Who are we? Who are we? We are the boys and girls of the Eastern and Western hemispheres, and we are going to help her with her delirium!

So from then on manias were declared reprehensible,

And everybody tried to be sensible,

And there wasn't any more war,

And there were only as many people dancing at night clubs as could comfortably get on the floor.

And all the rich people cried Soak the rich, and all the poor people cried No that would retard recovery, soak the poor!

And the tailors made men's and women's coats with the buttons on the same side, and that stopped a lot of argument between husbands and wives as to the comparative intelligence of men and women, you may be sure.

And what with one thing and another everybody was sensible and lived happily ever after and they said they owed it all to Miriam,

So they offered her the dictatorship of the world, but she never used it, only in a delirium.

THE TALE OF CUSTARD THE DRAGON

Belinda lived in a little white house,
With a little black kitten and a little gray mouse,
And a little yellow dog and a little red wagon,
And a realio, trulio, little pet dragon.

Now the name of the little black kitten was Ink,
And the little gray mouse, she called her Blink,
And the little yellow dog was sharp as Mustard,
But the dragon was a coward, and she called him Custard.

Custard the dragon had big sharp teeth,
And spikes on top of him and scales underneath,
Mouth like a fireplace, chimney for a nose,
And realio, trulio daggers on his toes.

Belinda was as brave as a barrel full of bears,
And Ink and Blink chased lions down the stairs,

Mustard was as brave as a tiger in a rage,
But Custard cried for a nice safe cage.

Belinda tickled him, she tickled him unmerciful,
Ink, Blink and Mustard, they rudely called him Percival,
They all sat laughing in the little red wagon
At the realio, trulio, cowardly dragon.

Belinda giggled till she shook the house,
And Blink said Weeck! which is giggling for a mouse,
Ink and Mustard rudely asked his age,
When Custard cried for a nice safe cage.

Suddenly, suddenly they heard a nasty sound,
And Mustard growled, and they all looked around.
Meowch! cried Ink, and Ooh! cried Belinda,
For there was a pirate, climbing in the winda.

Pistol in his left hand, pistol in his right,
And he held in his teeth a cutlass bright,
His beard was black, one leg was wood;
It was clear that the pirate meant no good.

Belinda paled, and she cried Help! Help!
But Mustard fled with a terrified yelp,
Ink trickled down to the bottom of the household,
And little mouse Blink strategically mouseholed.

But up jumped Custard, snorting like an engine,
Clashed his tail like irons in a dungeon,
With a clatter and a clank and a jangling squirm
He went at the pirate like a robin at a worm.

The pirate gaped at Belinda's dragon,
And gulped some grog from his pocket flagon,
He fired two bullets, but they didn't hit,
And Custard gobbled him, every bit.

Belinda embraced him, Mustard licked him,
No one mourned for his pirate victim.
Ink and Blink in glee did gyrate
Around the dragon that ate the pyrate.

Belinda still lives in her little white house,
With her little black kitten and her little gray mouse,
And her little yellow dog and her little red wagon,
And her realio, trulio, little pet dragon.

Belinda is as brave as a barrel full of bears,
And Ink and Blink chase lions down the stairs,
Mustard is as brave as a tiger in a rage,
But Custard keeps crying for a nice safe cage.

ELECTRA BECOMES MORBID

I

Abandon for a moment, friends,
Your frivolous means, your futile ends;
Life is not wholly beer and skittles,
A treasure hunt for love and victuals;
And so at times I think we ought
To pause and think a sobering thought.
Myself, I feel a dark despair

When I consider human hair.
I'm chicken-hearted, beetle-browed,
As I behold the heedless crowd,
Knowing each carefree individual
The slave of hair that runs on schidual.
On every human head or chin
It's falling out or growing in.
Yon whistling adolescent scholar,
Released from Ye Olde Tonsorial Parlor,
Runs up his neck with fingers tense
Like sticks along a picket fence.
His scalp is all Bay Rum and bristles,
Therefore he's pleased and therefore whistles.
Yea, he rejoices, quite unknowing
That all the time his hair is growing.
O woe is you, unhappy scholar,
Next month you'll be back in the tonsorial parlor.

II

Myself I feel a dark despair,
When I consider human hair
(Fine filaments sprouting from the skin),
I tremble like an aspirin.
For men and women everywhere
Unconsciously are growing hair,
Or, if the other hand you choose,
With every breath a hair they lose.
Unbid it cometh, likewise goeth,
And oftentimes it's doing boeth.
This habit is the chief determinant
Why permanent waves are less than permanent.

You rise, Madame, you face your mirror,
You utter cries of shame and terror.
What though to males you look all right?
For heaven's sake, your hair's a sight.
You hasten to the Gallic lair
Where lurks Maurice, or Jean or Pierre.
Between arrival and departure
You suffer hours of vicious torture,
At last emerging, white and weak,
But sure at least your mane is chic.
Thus you rejoice, my dear, unknowing
That all the time your hair is growing.
The waves so dearly purchasèd
Next month will have grown a foot or so away from your
    head.

III

I've said, I think, I think we ought
To think at times a sobering thought.
Man's lot it is to be a field
For crops that no nutrition yield,
That filter through his tender skin
And ripen on his head or chin. .
I face mankind and shudder, knowing
That everybody's hair is growing;
That lovers, linked in darkened hallways,
Are capped with hair that groweth always;
That millions, shaven in the morning,
At eve find beards their jowls adorning;
That hair is creeping through the scalps
Of yodelers yodeling in the Alps,

And pushing through the epidermises
Of peasants frolicking at kermises;
And poking bravely through the pores
Of cannibals on tropic shores;
That freezing, scorching, raining, snowing,
People's hair is always growing.
I contemplate with dark despair
The awful force of growing hair,
Although admitting, to be quite honest,
That it will be worth a million Niagaras to humanity if
    Science can ever get it harnessed.

BANKERS ARE JUST LIKE ANYBODY ELSE, EXCEPT RICHER

This is a song to celebrate banks,
Because they are full of money and you go into them and
    all you hear is clinks and clanks,
Or maybe a sound like the wind in the trees on the hills,
Which is the rustling of the thousand-dollar bills.
Most bankers dwell in marble halls,
Which they get to dwell in because they encourage de-
    posits and discourage withdralls,
And particularly because they all observe one rule which
    woe betides the banker who fails to heed it,
Which is you must never lend any money to anybody
    unless they don't need it.
O you cautious conservative banks, what I know about
    you!
If people are worried about their rent it is your duty to
    deny them the loan of one Confederate sou;

But suppose people come in and they have a million and
     they want another million to pile on top of it,
Why, you brim with the milk of human kindness and
     you urge them to accept every drop of it,
And you lend them the million so then they have two
     million and this gives them the idea that they would
     be better off with four,
So they already have two million as security so you have
     no hesitation in lending them two more,
And all the vice-presidents nod their heads in rhythm,
And the only question asked is Do the borrowers want
     the money sent or do they want to take it withm?
But please do not think that I am not fond of banks,
Because I think they deserve our appreciation and thanks,
Because they perform a valuable public service in elimi-
     nating the jackasses who go around saying that
     health and happiness are everything and money isn't
     essential,
Because as soon as they have to borrow some unimpor-
     tant money to maintain their health and happiness
     they starve to death so they can't go around any
     more sneering at good old money, which is nothing
     short of providential.

THE CALF

Pray, butcher, spare yon tender calf!
Accept my plea on his behalf;
He's but a babe, too young by far
To perish in the abattoir.
Oh, cruel butcher, let him feed

And gambol on the verdant mead;
Let clover tops and grassy banks
Fill out those childish ribs and flanks.
Then may we, at some future meal,
Pitch into beef, instead of veal.

A CLEAN CONSCIENCE NEVER RELAXES

There is an emotion to which we are most of us adduced,
But it is one which I refuse to boost.
It is harrowing, browbeating, and brutal,
Besides which it is futile.
I am referring, of course,
To remorse.
Remorse is a violent dyspepsia of the mind,
But it is very difficult to treat because it cannot even be
    defined,
Because everything is not gold that glisters and every-
    thing is not a tear that glistens,
And one man's remorse is another man's reminiscence,
So the truth is that as far as improving the world is con-
    cerned, remorse is a duffer,
Because the wrong people suffer,
Because the very fact that they suffer from remorse proves
    they are innocuous,
Yes indeed, it is the man remorse passes over completely
    who is the virulent streptococcuous.
Do you think that when Nero threw a martyr to the lions
    remorse enveloped him like an affinity?
Why, the only remorse in the whole Colosseum was felt
    by the martyr who was probably reproaching him-

self for having dozed through the sermon on the
   second Sunday after Trinity.
So I think remorse ought to stop biting the consciences
   that feed it,
And I think the Communist Party ought to work out
   some plan for taking it away from those who have
   it and giving it to those who need it.

APARTMENT TO SUBLET—UNFURNISHED

The Murrays are hunting a house,
They are tired of living in flats.
They long for a personal mouse,
And a couple of personal cats.
They are hunting a house to inhabit,
An Eden, or even an Arden,
They are thinking of keeping a rabbit,
They are thinking of digging a garden.
How giddy the Murrays have grown,
To aspire to a house of their own!

Oh, hurry, hurry!
Says Mrs. Murray.
Tarry awhile, says he,
If you care for a house
As is a house,
You'd better leave it to me.
I'd like an orchard, apple or peach,
I'd like an accessible bathing beach,
And a den for unwinding detective plots,
And a lawn for practising mashie shots,

And open fires,
And a pleasant sunroom,
A handy garage,
And perhaps a gunroom,
And an atmosphere exempt of static,
And a furnace silent and automatic.
For such a house
I would hurry, hurry —
I'm a practical man,
Says Mr. Murray.

The Murrays of 17 B,
The Murrays are going away,
From the wireless in 17 C,
And the parties in 17 A.
For the Murrays are tired of flats,
They are rapidly growing aloof,
As they dream of their personal cats,
As they dream of their personal roof.
Their friends cannot smother their merriment
When they speak of the Murrays' experiment.

Oh, hurry, hurry!
Says Mr. Murray.
Tarry awhile, says she.
When we choose a house,
Let us choose a house
As nice as a house can be.
With a dozen windows South and East,
And a dozen capacious cupboards at least,
And a laundry lilting with light and air,
And a porch for a lady to dry her hair,

And plenty of sun,
And plenty of shade,
And a neat little place
For a neat little maid,
And a wall with roses clambering wild,
And a quiet room for a sleepy child.
If you happen to see it,
Hurry, hurry!
For that's the house,
Says Mrs. Murray.

I HAVE IT ON GOOD AUTHORITY

There are two kinds of people who blow through life
    like a breeze,
And one kind is gossipers, and the other kind is gos-
    sipees.
And they certainly annoy each other,
But they certainly enjoy each other,
Yes, they pretend to flout each other,
But they couldn't do without each other,
Because gossipers are lost without a thrill and a shock,
Because they like to sit in rocking chairs and gossip
    and rock and rock and gossip and gossip and rock,
And if the gossipees weren't there to give them a thrill
    and a shock their life would be all rocking and no
    gossip,
Which would be as flat as music without people named
    Sacha and Yehudi and Ossip,
While on the other hand everybody errs

If they think the gossipees could be happy without the gossipers,

Because you don't have to study under Freud or Adler or Coué

To know that it isn't any fun being a roué if nobody notices that you are a roué,

And indeed connoisseurs agree

That even gossipers don't know anything about gossip until they have heard one gossipee gossiping about another gossipee.

Another good thing about gossip is that it is within everybody's reach,

And it is much more interesting than any other form of speech,

Because suppose you eschew gossip and just say Mr. Smith is in love with his wife,

Why that disposes of the Smiths as a topic of conversation for the rest of their life,

But suppose you say with a smile, that poor little Mrs. Smith thinks her husband is in love with her, he must be very clever,

Why then you can enjoyably talk about the Smiths forever.

So a lot of people go around determined not to hear and not to see and not to speak any evil,

And I say Pooh for them, are you a man or a mouse, are you a woman or a weevil?

And I also say Pooh for sweetness and light,

And if you want to get the most out of life why the thing to do is to be a gossiper by day and a gossipee by night.

What am I doing, daughter mine?
A-haying while the sun doth shine;
Gathering rosebuds while I may
To hoard against a barren day;
Reveling in the brief sensation
Of basking in your admiration.
Oh, now, when you are almost five
I am the lordliest man alive;
Your gaze is blind to any flaw,
And brimming with respect and awe.
You think me handsome, strong and brave,
You come at morn to watch me shave.
The neighbors' insults lose their sting
When you encourage me to sing,
And like a fashion plate I pose
While you compliment my clothes.
Who wishes his self-esteem to thrive
Should belong to a girl of almost five.
But almost five can't last forever,
And wide-eyed girls grow tall and clever.
Few creatures others less admire
Than a lass of seventeen her sire.
What humiliation must you weather
When we are seen in public together!
Perchance I'll munch a stick of gum,
Or in the theater brazenly hum;
My hat, belike, will flout the law
Laid down for hats at Old Nassau;
My anecdotes you'll strive to stanch,
And at my table manners blanch;

My every word and every deed
Will agony and embarrassment breed;
Your goal of goals, the end of your ends,
To hide me forever from your friends.
Therefore I now chant roundelays,
And rollick in your pride and praise;
Too soon the nymph that you will be
Will shudder when she looks at me.

FUNEBRIAL REFLECTION

Among the anthropophagi
People's friends are people's sarcophagi.

THE STRANGE CASE OF MR. FORTAGUE'S DISAPPOINTMENT

Once upon a time there was a man named Mr. Lionel
Fortague.

∾

He didn't have very much to talk about.

∾

In summer he used to ask people if it was hot enough
for them.

∾

It always was.

∾

In winter he used to ask people if it was cold enough for
them.

∾

It always was.

ოფ

Mr. Lionel Fortague got pretty sick of people it was hot enough for.

ოფ

He got pretty sick of people it was cold enough for, too.

ოფ

He decided he would arise and go now.

ოფ

He decided he would go to Innisfree.

ოფ

The people of Innisfree are different, thought Mr. Lionel Fortague.

ოფ

As soon as he got to Innisfree he asked the people if it was cold enough for them.

ოფ

They asked him What? Was what cold enough for who?

ოფ

Mr. Lionel Fortague was delighted.

ოფ

I knew Innisfree would be different, he said to himself.

ოფ

He could hardly wait for summer to verify his conclusion.

ოფ

As soon as summer came he asked everybody if it was hot enough for them.

ოფ

Everybody said the question was familiar but they couldn't remember the answer.

ოფ

Mr. Lionel Fortague said he would settle down on Innisfree, the home of iridescent chitchat.

ოფ

He said he would a small cabin build there, of clay and
    wattles made.

◦◦◦

Everybody said Did he mean he would build a small
    cabin there, made of clay and wattles?

◦◦◦

Mr. Lionel Fortague said yes, but his way of putting it
    was more poetic.

◦◦◦

Everybody said Maybe, but they were all out of wattles.

◦◦◦

Mr. Lionel Fortague grew very angry at the people of
    Innisfree.

◦◦◦

He a small cabin built there, of clay and beaverboard
    made.

◦◦◦

He a fierce-looking dog at an annual clearance sale
    bought, and it the people of Innisfree one by one
    to bite he instructed.

◦◦◦

My, he was disappointed.

◦◦◦

He had forgotten that a bargain dog never bites.

THE PARTY

Come Arabella, fetch the cake,
On a dish with silver handles.
Oh mercy! Feel the table shake!
Lucinda, light the candles.

· 255 ·

For Mr. Migg is thir-ty,
Is thir—ty,
Is thir——ty.
The years are crawling over him
Like wee red ants.
Oh, three times ten is thir-ty,
Is for—ty,
Is fif——ty.
The further off from England
The nearer is to France.

The little flames they bob and jig,
The dining hall is breezy.
Quick! puff your candles, Mr. Migg,
The little flames die easy.
For Mr. Migg is for-ty,
Is for—ty,
Is for——ty.
The years are crawling over him
Like wee red ants.
Oh four times ten is for-ty,
Is fif—ty,
Is six——ty,
And creeping through the icing,
The other years advance.

Why, Arabella, here's a ring!
Lucinda, here's a thimble!
For Mr. Migg there's not a thing —
'Tis not, I trust, a symbol!

For Mr. Migg is fif-ty,
Is fif—ty,

Is fif——ty.
The years are crawling over him
Like wee red ants.
Oh, five times ten is fif-ty,
Is six—ty,
Is seven——ty.
Lucinda, put the cake away.
We're going to the dance.

CURL UP AND DIET

Some ladies smoke too much and some ladies drink too
    much and some ladies pray too much,
But all ladies think that they weigh too much.
They may be as slender as a sylph or a dryad,
But just let them get on the scales and they embark on
    a doleful jeremiad;
No matter how low the figure the needle happens to
    touch,
They always claim it is at least five pounds too much;
No matter how underfed to you a lady's anatomy
    seemeth,
She describes herself as Leviathan or Behemoth;
To the world she may appear slinky and feline,
But she inspects herself in the mirror and cries, Oh, I
    look like a sea lion.
Once upon a time there was a girl more beautiful and
    witty and charming than tongue can tell,
And she is now a dangerous raving maniac in a padded
    cell,

And the first indication her friends and relatives had that
    she was mentally overwrought
Was one day when she said, I weigh a hundred and
    twenty-seven, which is exactly what I ought.
Oh, often I am haunted
By the thought that somebody might some day discover
    a diet that would let ladies reduce just as much as
    they wanted,
Because I wonder if there is a woman in the world strong-
    minded enough to shed ten pounds or twenty,
And say There now, that's plenty;
And I fear me one ten-pound loss would only arouse the
    craving for another,
So it wouldn't do any good for ladies to get their ambi-
    tion and look like somebody's fourteen-year-old
    brother,
Because, having accomplished this with ease,
They would next want to look like somebody's fourteen-
    year-old brother in the final stages of some obscure
    disease,
And the more success you have the more you want to
    get of it,
So then their goal would be to look like somebody's
    fourteen-year-old brother's ghost, or rather not the
    ghost itself, which is fairly solid, but a silhouette
    of it,
So I think it is very nice for ladies to be lithe and lissome,
But not so much so that you cut yourself if you happen
    to embrace or kissome.

REFLECTIONS ON ICE-BREAKING

Candy
Is dandy
But liquor
Is quicker.

THE PASSIONATE PAGAN AND THE DISPASSIONATE PUBLIC

A TRAGEDY OF THE MACHINE AGE

Boys and girls,
Come out to play,
The moon is shining
Bright as day.

If the moon is shining
Bright as day,
We think that we'll
Stay in and play.

Hey nonny nonny!
Come, Jennie! Come, Johnnie!
The year's adolescent!
The air's effervescent!
It bubbles like Schweppes!
Aren't you going to take steppes?

It's one of the commoner
Vernal phenomena.
You may go wild

Over air that is mild,
But Johnnie and Jennie
Are not having any.

It is Spring! It is Spring!
Let us leap! Let us sing!
Let us claim we have hives
And abandon our wives!
Let us hire violins
To belittle our sins!
Let us loll in a grotto!
Let this be our motto:
Not sackcloth, but satin!
Not Nordic, but Latin!

An epicene voice
Is our amorous choice!
Tell us that Luna
Compares with that cruna.
Away with your capers!
Go peddle your papers!

It is Spring! It is Spring!
On the lea, on the ling!
The frost is dispersed!
Like the buds let us burst!
Let the sap in our veins
Rush like limited trains!
Let our primitive urges
Disgruntle our clergies,
While Bacchus and Pan
Cavort in the van!

Spring is what winter
Always gazinta.
Science finds reasons
For mutable seasons.
Can't you react
With a little more tact?
Please go and focus
Your whims on a crocus.

It is Spring! Is it Spring?
Let us sing! Shall we sing?
On the lea, on the ling
Shall we sing it is Spring?
Will nobody fling
A garland to Spring?
Oh, hey nonny nonny!
Oh, Jennie! Oh, Johnnie!
Doesn't dove rhyme with love
While the moon shines above?
Isn't May for the wooer
And June for l'amour?
No, it couldn't be Spring!
Do not dance! Do not sing!
These birds and these flowers,
These breezes and bowers,
These gay tirra-lirras
Are all done with mirrors!
Hey nonny! Hey nonny!
Hey nonny! Hey nonny!
Hey nonny! Hey nonny!
Hey nonny . . .

CAPTAIN JOHN SMITH

Captain John Smith
Didn't belong to the B'nai B'rith,
He was a full-blooded Briton,
The same as Boadicea and Bulwer-Lytton,
But his problem and theirs were not quite the same,
Because they didn't have to go around assuring every-
    body that that was their real name,
And finally he said, This business of everybody raising
    their eyebrows when I register at an inn is getting
    very boring,
So I guess I'll go exploring,
So he went and explored the River James,
Where they weren't as particular then as they are now
    about names,
And he went for a walk in the forest,
And the Indians caught him and my goodness wasn't he
    emborrassed!
And he was too Early American to write for advice from
    Emily Post,
So he prepared to give up the ghost,
And he prayed a prayer but I don't know whether it was
    a silent one or a vocal one,
Because the Indians were going to dash his brains out
    and they weren't going to give him an anæsthetic,
    not even a local one,
But along came Pocahontas and she called off her fa-
    ther's savage minions,
Because she was one of the most prominent Virginians,
And her eyes went flash flash,
And she said, Scat, you po' red trash,

And she begged Captain John Smith's pardon,
And she took him for a walk in the gyarden,
And she said, Ah reckon ah sho' would have felt bad if
    anything had happened to you-all,
And she told him about her great-uncle Hiawatha and
    her cousin Sittin' Bull and her kissin' cousin King
    Philip, and I don't know who-all,
And he said you'd better not marry me, you'd better
    marry John Rolfe,
So he bade her farewell and went back to England, which
    adjoins Scotland, where they invented golf.

TO A SMALL BOY STANDING ON MY SHOES
WHILE I AM WEARING THEM

Let's straighten this out, my little man,
And reach an agreement if we can.
I entered your door as an honored guest.
My shoes are shined and my trousers are pressed,
And I won't stretch out and read you the funnies
And I won't pretend that we're Easter bunnies.
If you must get somebody down on the floor,
What in the hell are your parents for?
I do not like the things that you say
And I hate the games that you want to play.
No matter how frightfully hard you try,
We've little in common, you and I.
The interest I take in my neighbor's nursery
Would have to grow, to be even cursory,
And I would that performing sons and nephews
Were carted away with the daily refuse,

And I hold that frolicsome daughters and nieces
Are ample excuse for breaking leases.
You may take a sock at your daddy's tummy
Or climb all over your doting mummy,
But keep your attentions to me in check
Or, sonny boy, I will wring your neck.
A happier man today I'd be
Had someone wrung it ahead of me.

SUMMERGREEN FOR PRESIDENT

Winter is indeed a season that I would like to apply an uncomplimentary name to,

But I really don't mind it as much as the people who enjoy it, or at least claim to.

Yes, some people still say ice is nicer than slush,

And to those people I say Hush.

Some people still say snow is nicer than rain,

Which is like being still unreconciled to the defeat of James G. Blaine.

Some people still say a freeze is nicer than a thaw,

And I hope they find cold-storage Japanese beetles in their slaw.

Slush is much nicer than ice because when you step in it you simply go splash, instead of immediately depositing either your posterior or your pate on it,

And also you don't have to skate on it.

Rain is much nicer than snow because you don't have to have rain plows piling rain up in six-foot piles exactly where you want to go,

And you don't have to build rain-men for the kiddies and
frolic in sleighs and sleds, and also rain is nicer because it melts the snow.
A thaw is obviously much nicer than a freeze,
Because it annoys people with skis.
And in all my life I have only known one man who
honestly liked winter better than summer,
Because every summer he used to have either his tonsils
or his appendix or something out, and every winter
he was a plumber.

CONFESSIONS OF A BORN SPECTATOR

One infant grows up and becomes a jockey,
Another plays basketball or hockey.
This one the prize ring hastes to enter,
That one becomes a tackle or center.
I'm just as glad as glad can be
That I'm not them, that they're not me.

With all my heart do I admire
Athletes who sweat for fun or hire,
Who take the field in gaudy pomp
And maim each other as they romp;
My limp and bashful spirit feeds
On other people's heroic deeds.

Now A runs ninety yards to score;
B knocks the champion to the floor;
C, risking vertebrae and spine,

Lashes his steed across the line.
You'd think my ego it would please
To swap positions with one of these.

Well, ego might be pleased enough,
But zealous athletes play so rough;
They do not ever, in their dealings,
Consider one another's feelings.
I'm glad that when my struggle begins
Twixt prudence and ego, prudence wins.

When swollen eye meets gnarlèd fist,
When snaps the knee, and cracks the **wrist,**
When calm officialdom demands,
Is there a doctor in the stands?
My soul in true thanksgiving speaks
For this most modest of physiques.

Athletes, I'll drink to you or eat with you,
Or anything except compete with you;
Buy tickets worth their weight in radium
To watch you gambol in a stadium,
And reassure myself anew
That you're not me and I'm not you.

THE PIG

The pig, if I am not mistaken,
Supplies us sausage, ham, and bacon.
Let others say his heart is big —
I call it stupid of the pig.

A DRINK WITH SOMETHING IN IT

There is something about a Martini,
A tingle remarkably pleasant;
A yellow, a mellow Martini;
I wish that I had one at present.
There is something about a Martini,
Ere the dining and dancing begin,
And to tell you the truth,
It is not the vermouth —
I think that perhaps it's the Gin.

There is something about an old-fashioned
That kindles a cardiac glow;
It is soothing and soft and impassioned
As a lyric by Swinburne or Poe.
There is something about an old-fashioned
When dusk has enveloped the sky,
And it may be the ice,
Or the pineapple slice,
But I strongly suspect it's the Rye.

There is something about a mint julep.
It is nectar imbibed in a dream,
As fresh as the bud of the tulip,
As cool as the bed of the stream.
There is something about a mint julep,
A fragrance beloved by the lucky.
And perhaps it's the tint
Of the frost and the mint,
But I think it was born in Kentucky.

There is something they put in a highball
That awakens the torpidest brain,
That kindles a spark in the eyeball,
Gliding singing through vein after vein.
There is something they put in a highball
Which you'll notice one day, if you watch;
And it may be the soda,
But judged by the odor,
I rather believe it's the Scotch.

Then here's to the heartening wassail,
Wherever good fellows are found;
Be its master instead of its vassal,
And order the glasses around.
Oh, it's Beer if you're bent on expansion,
And Wine if you wish to grow thin,
But quaffers who think
Of a drink as a drink,
When they quaff, quaff of Whisky and Gin.

"MY CHILD IS PHLEGMATIC . . ."
—ANXIOUS PARENT

Anxious Parent, I guess you have just never been around;
I guess you just don't know who are the happiest people
       anywhere to be found;
So you are worried, are you, because your child is turning
       out to be phlegmatic?
Forgive me if I seem a trifle unsympathetic.
Why do you want your child to be a flashing, coruscat-
       ing gem?

· 268 ·

Don't you know the only peace the world can give lies
    not in flame but in phlegm?
Don't you know that the people with souls of putty
Are the only people who are sitting prutty?
They never get all worked up at the drop of a pin or a
    feather or a hat,
They never go around saying bitterly to themselves: "Oh
    God, did I really do, did I really say that?"
They never boil over when they read about stool pigeons
    getting girls into reformatories by making treacher-
    ous advances;
They never get perfectly futilely harrowed about Sacco
    and Vanzetti, or Alice Adamses who don't have
    good times at dances;
They never blink an eyelash about colleges that are going
    to the dogs because of football overemphasis;
They never almost die with indignation when some
    colored person is lynched in Natchez or Memphasis.
No, when they eat they digest their food, and when they
    go to bed they get right to sleep,
And four phlegmatic angels a stolid watch over them
    keep.
Oh to be phlegmatic, oh to be stolid, oh to be torpid, oh
    to be calm!
For it is only thus, Anxious Parent, that we can get
    through life without a qualm.

THE COBRA

This creature fills its mouth with venum
And walks upon its duodenum.

He who attempts to tease the cobra
Is soon a sadder he, and sobra.

LET ME BUY THIS ONE

Solomon said, Stay me with apples for I am sick with
l'amour,
But I say, Comfort me with flagons, for I am sick with
rich people talking and acting poor.
I have never yet met even a minor Crœsus
Whose pocketbook didn't have paresis;
I have never yet been out with a tycoon for an evening
in Manhattan's glamorous canyons
When the evening's bills weren't paid by the tycoon's
impoverished but proud companions.
There is one fact of life that no unwealthy child can
learn too soon,
Which is that no tycoon ever spends money except on
another tycoon.
Rich people are people that you owe something to and
take out to dinner and the theater and dancing and
all the other expensive things there are because you
know they are accustomed to the best and as a result you spend the following month on your uppers,
And it is a big evening to you but just another evening
to them and they return the hospitality by saying
that someday you must drop in to one of their cold
Sunday suppers.
Rich people are also people who spend most of their
time complaining about the income tax as one of
life's greatest and most intolerable crosses,

And eventually you find that they haven't even paid any
income tax since 1929 because their income has
shrunk to fifty thousand dollars a year and everything has been charged off to losses,

And your own income isn't income at all, it is salary, and
stops coming in as soon as you stop laboring mentally
and manually,

But you have been writing out checks for the Government annually,

So the tax situation is just the same as the entertainment
situation because the poor take their little pittance

And pay for the rich's admittance

Because it is a great truth that as soon as people have
enough coupons in the safe-deposit vault or in the
cookie-jar on the shelf,

Why they don't have to pay anything themself,

No, they can and do just take all their coins and store
them,

And other people beg to pay for everything for them,

And they certainly are allowed to,

Because to accept favors is the main thing that the poor
are and the rich aren't too proud to,

So let us counterattack with sangfroid and phlegm,

And I propose a Twenty-second Amendment to the Con-
stitution providing that the rich must spend as much
money on us poor as we do on them.

RAINY DAY

Linell is clad in a gown of green,
She walks in state like a fairy queen.

Her train is tucked in a winsome bunch
Directly behind her royal lunch.
With a dignified skip and a haughty hop
Her golden slippers go clippety-clop.
I think I am Mummy, says Linell.
I'm Mummy too, says Isabel.

Linell has discovered a filmy veil;
The very thing for a swishy tail.
The waves wash over the nursery floor
And break on the rug with a rumbling roar;
The swishy tail gives a swishy swish;
She's off and away like a frightened fish.
Now I'm a mermaid, says Linell.
I'm mermaid too, says Isabel.

Her trousers are blue, her hair is kinky,
Her jacket is red and her skin is inky.
She is hiding behind a green umbrella;
She couldn't be Alice, or Cinderella,
Or Puss in Boots, or the Fiddlers Three;
Goodness gracious, who can she be?
I'm Little Black Sambo, says Linell.
I'm Sambo, too, says Isabel.

Clack the shutters. The blinds are drawn.
Click the switch, and the lights are gone.
Linell is under the blankets deep,
Murmuring down the hill to sleep.
Oh, deep in the soft and gentle dark
She stirs and chirps like a drowsy lark.
I love you, Mummy, says Linell.
Love Mummy too, says Isabel.

MY DADDY

I have a funny daddy
Who goes in and out with me,
And everything that baby does
My daddy's sure to see,
And everything that baby says
My daddy's sure to tell.
You must have read my daddy's verse.
I hope he fries in hell.

CAT NAPS ARE TOO GOOD FOR CATS

Oh, early every afternoon
I like a temporary swoon.
I do not overeat at luncheon,
I do not broach the bowl or puncheon;
Yet the hour from two to three
Is always sleepy-time to me.

Bolt upright at my desk I sit,
My elbows digging into it,
My chin into my hands doth fit,
My careful fingers screen my eyes,
And all my work before me lies,
Which leads inquisitive passer-bys
Who glance my way and see me nod,
To think me wide awake, if odd.

I would not sell my daily swoon
For all the rubies in Rangoon.

What! sell my swoon? My lovely swoon?
Oh, many and many's the afternoon
I've scoured the woods with Daniel Boone,
And sipped a julep with Lorna Doone,
I'll sell my soul before my swoon,
It's not for sale, my swoon's immune.

From two to three each afternoon
Mine are the Mountains of the Moon,
Mine a congenital silver spoon.
And I can lead a lost platoon
Or dive for pearls in a haunted lagoon,
Or guide a stratosphere balloon.
Oh, where the schooner schoons, I schoon,
I can talk lion, or baboon,
Or make a crooner cease to croon.
I like to swoon, for when I swoon
The universe is my macaroon.

Then blessings on thee, my afternoon torpor,
Thou makest a prince of a mental porpor.

THE STRANGE CASE OF THE PLEASING
TAXI-DRIVER

Once upon a time there was a taxi-driver named Llewellyn Abdullah — White — Male — 5-10½ — 170.

∽

Llewellyn had promised his mother he would be the best
taxi-driver in the world.

∽

His mother was in heaven.

⁓

At least, she was in a Fool's Paradise because her boy
was the best taxi-driver in the world.

⁓

He was, too.

⁓

He called his male passengers Sir instead of Mac, and
his female passengers Madam instead of Sister.

⁓

On rainy nights his flag was always up.

⁓

He knew not only how to find the Waldorf, but the
shortest route to 5954 Gorsuch Avenue.

⁓

He said Thank you when tipped, and always had change
for five dollars.

⁓

He never drove with a cigar in his mouth, lighted or un-
lighted.

⁓

If you asked him to please not drive so fast, he drove not
so fast, and didn't get mad about it, either.

⁓

He simply adored traffic cops, and he was polite to Sunday drivers.

⁓

When he drove a couple through the park he never
looked back and he never eavesdropped.

⁓

My boy is the best taxi-driver in the world and no eaves-
dropper, said his mother.

⁓

The only trouble was that the bad taxi-drivers got all the
business.

❧

Llewellyn shrank from White — Male — 5-10½ — 170
to Sallow — Male — 5-9¾ — 135.

❧

Cheest, Llewellyn, said his mother.

❧

Cheest, Mother, replied Llewellyn.

❧

Llewellyn and his mother understood each other.

❧

He took his last five dollars in dimes and nickels which
he had been saving for change and spent it on cigars
at two for a nickel.

❧

The next day he insulted seven passengers and a traffic
cop, tore the fender off a car from Enid, Oklahoma,
and passed through 125th Street while taking a dear
old lady from 52nd to 58th.

❧

That evening he had forty dollars on the clock.

❧

Llewellyn is no longer the best taxi-driver in the world,
but his license reads White — Male — 5-11 — 235.

❧

In the park he is the father of all eavesdroppers.

❧

Couples who protest find him adamant.

❧

Since he is the father of all eavesdroppers and adamant,
I think we might call him an Adam-ant-Eves-
dropper and there leave him.

❧

Good-by, Llewellyn.

BENJAMIN

There was a brave girl of Connecticut
Who flagged the express with her pecticut,
Which her elders defined
As presence of mind,
But deplorable absence of ecticut.

THE CITY

This beautiful ditty
Is, for a change, about the city,
Although ditties aren't very popular
Unless they're rural and not metropular.

Sentimentalists object to towns initially
Because they are made artificially,
But so is vaccination,
While smallpox is an original creation.

Artists speak of everything urban
As the W.C.T.U. speaks of rye and bourbon,
And they say cities are only commercial marts,
But they fail to realize that no marts, no arts.

The country was made first,
Yes, but people lived in it and rehearsed,
And when they finally got civilization down,
Why, they moved to town.

City people always want the most faucets
And the comfortablest caucets,

And labor-saving devices in their kitchenette,
And at the movies, armchairs in which to set.

Take country people, they suffer stoically,
But city people prefer to live unheroically;
Therefore city dentistry is less painful,
Because city dentists find it more gainful.

City people are querulous and queasy,
And they'd rather die than not live easy;
And if they did die, they'd find fault
If they weren't put in an air-conditioned vault.

Yes, indeed, they are certainly sissies,
Not at all like Hercules or Ulysses.
But because they are so soft,
City life is comfortable, if not perpetually, at least oft.

A GOOD PARENT'S GARDEN OF VISION

Part I: The Dream

In my bachelor days, no parent I,
My spirits fell as the weeks ran by,
And, tossing on my pallet, I dolefully thought
Of Time, the tri-motored Juggernaut,
Or paused at whiles amid my gardening
To listen for the sound of my arteries hardening.
But now I eagerly listen for
Senility knocking at the door.
You ask, and properly ask, no doubt,

Whence this astonishing right-about?
Why now so Frances Hodgson Bùrnett-y? —
Not Pelmanism, but paternity.
Come dotage, envelop me in your arms,
Old age, I ween, has its special charms.
I'll camp awhile by Jordan's water
And enjoy being a nuisance to my daughter.
The loving offspring of Mr. N.
Won't trouble her head with raw young men,
Young men who cry she is lissome and flowery,
Young men who inquire about her dowery.
She'll make young men all keep their distances,
She'll listen to her father's reministances,
She'll fondly lay out his favorite slippers,
And when he wears arctics she'll zip his zippers,
She'll nogg his eggs and she'll toast his kippers,
And disparage the quips of the current quippers.
She'll light his pipe and she'll mix his drinks
And conceal from her father every thought she thinks,
And he in his way and she in hern
Will be merry as a melody by Mr. Kern.

Part II: The Nightmare

And he in his way and she in hern
Will be merry as ashes in a funeral urn.
She'll discourage his pipe and she'll hide his drinks,
And she'll tell her father every thought she thinks.
She'll make audible comments on his taste in togs,
She'll put his eggs in custards and not in noggs,
She'll object to the odor of kippering kippers,
She will laugh Ha Ha! at the current quippers,

She will leave the room when he dons his slippers,
When his buttons unbutton she will advocate zippers.
She'll see that parents keep their proper distances,
And she'll give young men a lot of reministances,
She'll look at her father like a beetle from the Bowery,
And ask why she hasn't a decent dowery,
And the only moments she'll be really merry
Will be pricing plots at the cemetery,
And I fear by the time his epitaph's read,
She'll be either a spinster or five times wed.

Part III: The Awakening

O pleasing daughter of Mr. N.,
His forebodings are happily beyond your ken,
And I gravely doubt that his querulous words
Retard the digestion of your whey and curds,
For children all choose their own sweet way —
Say Disobey, and they Datobey.
It's not that they're all in the pay of Belial,
It's only their way of being filial.
Some grow up hideous, others beautiful,
Some ungrateful and others dutiful;
Why try to prognosticate which yours will be?
There's nothing to do but wait and see.
Only nasty parents lose their nerve
At the prospect of getting what they deserve.
With a conscience as clear as mountain water
I await the best from my loving daughter.

THE LAMA

The one-l lama,
He's a priest.
The two-l llama,
He's a beast.
And I will bet
A silk pajama
There isn't any
Three-l lllama.*

WAITING FOR THE BIRDIE

Some hate broccoli, some hate bacon,
I hate having my picture taken.
How can your family claim to love you
And then demand a picture of you?
The electric chair is a queasy chair,
But I know an equally comfortless pair;
One is the dentist's, my good sirs,
And the other is the photographer's.
Oh, the fly in all domestic ointments
Is affectionate people who make appointments
To have your teeth filled left and right,
Or your face reproduced in black and white.
You open the door and you enter the studio,
And you feel less cheerio than nudio.
The hard light shines like seventy suns,
And you know that your features are foolish ones.

* The author's attention has been called to a type of con-
flagration known as a three-alarmer. Pooh.

The photographer says, Natural, please,
And you cross your knees and uncross your knees.
Like a duke in a high society chronicle
The camera glares at you through its monocle
And you feel ashamed of your best attire,
Your nose itches, your palms perspire,
Your muscles stiffen, and all the while
You smile and smile and smile and smile.
It's over; you weakly grope for the door;
It's not; the photographer wants one more.
And if this experience you survive,
Wait, just wait till the proofs arrive.
You look like a drawing by Thurber or Bab,
Or a gangster stretched on a marble slab.
And all your dear ones, including your wife,
Say There he is, that's him to the life!
Some hate broccoli, some hate bacon,
But I hate having my picture taken.

THE QUEEN IS IN THE PARLOR

Let's go over to Lily's,
And we'll all play games;
We'll act like regular sillies,
We'll assume ridiculous names,
We'll embarrass the butler,
And shock the maids,
With some of our subtler
Sly charades.
Come along, come along to Lily's,
Effervescent incessantly Lily's,

Come along, come along to Lily's,
And we'll all play games.

Lily is loaded with strictures
And many a palpable hit
For people who won't draw pictures,
For people who won't be IT.
There are sharpened pencils
And virgin papers,
All the utensils
For mental capers.
Here's a new one! You're going to love it!
Just enter into the spirit of it!
The name of the game is, Who Is Whom?
Harold, you have to leave the room;
I hope a few minutes alone won't bore you;
We'll whistle when we are ready for you.
Amanda, sit on the chandelier;
You represent Eternity, dear;
Now let me think — Oh yes, Louise,
Stand on the sofa — on one leg, please;
You're Nelson — oh, it was Nelson's arm!
Well, a change of limbs lends whimsical charm.
George and Edward are Scrooge and Marley;
Pincus, you be Bonnie Prince Charlie.
Now, do I dare be Cleopatra?
No, really I don't! Why George, you flattra!
Everyone ready? This is fun!
Harold must guess us, every one,
And portray us all in a cartoon trim
While we each write a sonnet on him.
Hoo hoo, Harold! Hoo hoo! Hoo hoo!

Come in now, Harold, we're ready for you!
Hoo hoo, Harold! — Oh no! Not that!
Harold is missing, and so's his hat.

Let's go over to Lily's,
We'll all play games;
We'll bloom like daffy-down-dillies
And romp like Colonial Dames.
Come along, come along to Lily's,
Energetic æsthetically Lily's,
Come along, come along to Lily's,
The Queen of the Parlor Games!

DO SPHINXES THINK?

There is one thing I do not understand,
Which is how anybody successfully cuts the fingernails
    on their right hand,
Because it is easy to cut your left-hand fingernails, but
    with your right-hand fingernails, why you either
    have to let them grow ad infinitum,
Or else bitum.
Then there is another problem that keeps my brain work-
    ing in two twelve-hour shifts,
Which is Why doesn't the fact that everything that
    goes up must come down, apply to elevators, or as
    the Americans say, lifts?
You have been standing on the tenth floor waiting to
    descend to the ground floor since Bob Son of Battle
    was a pup,

And all you see is elevators going up, up, up,

And first your impatience, and eventually your curiosity,
grows keen,

When you see the same elevator going up a dozen times
without having been down in between.

Is there a fourth dimension known only to elevator at-
tendants,

Or do they, when they get to the top, glide across the
roof to the next building and there make their
descendance?

Whatever the secret is, to know it I should adore,

For I am tired of being marooned without my ten
favorite movie actresses on the tenth floor.

An answer to the third baffler, however, would make the
greatest difference in this dear old life o' mine,

Which is, ought I to hope to feel terrible, or to feel fine?

Because how can I tell which hope to nurse,

Because when I feel terrible I know that after a while
I'll feel better, and when I feel fine I know that after
a while I'll feel worse.

Is it better to feel terrible and know that pretty soon
you'll feel fine, or to feel fine and know that pretty
soon you'll feel terrible, that is the question,

And I am open to suggestion,

And when you consider further that probably nobody
can ever feel either fine or terrible anyhow, because
how can you feel fine when you know that you're
going to feel terrible or how can you feel terrible
et cetera it all grows very confusing,

So let's leave everything in the hands of Dorothy Dix
and Ted Husing.

TO A LADY PASSING TIME BETTER LEFT
UNPASSED

O lady of the lucent hair,
Why do you play at solitaire?
What imp, what demon misanthrope,
Prompted this session of lonely hope?
What boredom drives you, and great Lord!
How can such as you be bored?
The gleaming world awaits your eye
While you essay futility.
That mouth is shaped for livelier sport
Than paging of a pasteboard court —
Why, even the Red Knave longing lingers,
While Black Queens wait, in those white fingers.
See now the joy that lights your face
Squandered on some fortuitous ace,
Where formerly dark anger burned
When a five perverse would not be turned.
O, know you not, that darkling frown
Could topple Caesar's empire down;
That quick, bright joy, if flashed on men,
Could sudden build it up again?
Get up! Get up! Throw down the pack!
Rise in your gown of shining black!
Withdraw, my dear, while you are able
The slender feet from neath the table;
Remove from the regretful baize
The elbows curved in cunning ways.
Is there no game that pleasure brings
But fretting over painted things?
No gay, ecstatic end in view

But shuffle and begin anew?
Get up, I tell you, girl, get up!
Wine keeps not ever in the cup;
Music is mortal, comes a day
When the musicians will not play;
Even Love immortal, love undying,
Finds the loved one's Patience trying.
Let two-and-fifty rivals hiss me —
For God's sake, girl, come here and kiss me!

WHO UNDERSTANDS WHO ANYHOW?

There is one phase of life that I have never heard discussed in any seminar,
And that is that all women think men are funny and all men think that weminar.
Be the air the air of America or England or Japan,
It is full of husbands up in it saying, Isn't that just like a woman? And wives saying, Isn't that just like a man?
Well, it so happens that this is a unique fight,
Because both sides are right.
Although I must say, while the opportunity is seasonable,
That I do think that women would rather be right than be reasonable.
But anyhow each sex keeps on laughing at the other sex for not thinking the way they do,
Which is the cause of most domestic to-do and a-do,
Because breakfast is punctuated with spousely snorts,
Because husbands are jeering at their wives because they ignore the front page and read society and fashions,

and wives are jeering at their husbands because they
ignore the front page and read finance and sports,

And women think it is ridiculous of men to spend their
spare time reading a book or catching a fish or wield-
ing a racket or a putter, or getting tattooed,

And men think it is ridiculous of women to spend their
spare time talking about other women who aren't
there, or going from shop to shop trying everything
on and not intending to buy anything, or getting
manicured or shampooed.

And men also think that women have an easy time because all they have to do is look after the household,

And what does that amount to but keeping an eye on the
children and seeing that three meals a day are served
and not allowing any litter to collect that would
furnish a foothold for a mousehold?

And women also think that men have an easy time because all they have to do is sit in an office all day
long swapping stories and scratching up desks with
their heels,

And going out to restaurants and ordering everything
they like for their midday meals,

And there is one special point on which couples can
never agree when they think,

And that is, how much is enough to drink.

And oh yes, women like to resent the thought that they
think men think they are toys,

And men like to bask in the thought that they think
women think they are just big overgrown boys.

Well all these conflicting thoughts make for trouble at
times but on the whole it is a sound idea for men
and women to think different,

It is a topic upon which I am verbose and vociferant,
Because who was it who wrote of the miserable town
    where the girls were too boisterous and the boys were
    too girlsterous, was it Damon Runyon,
Or could it have been John Bunyan?
Well anyhow, that author had a gifted pen;
Because who would want to live in a world where the
    men all thought like women and the women all
    thought like men?
No, no, kind sirs, I will take all my hard-earned money,
And I will bet it on the nose of the tribe whose men and
    women continue to think each other are funny.

THE PARENT

Children aren't happy with nothing to ignore,
And that's what parents were created for.

PARSLEY FOR VICE-PRESIDENT!

I'd like to be able to say a good word for parsley, but I
    can't,
And after all what can you find to say for something that
    even the dictionary dismisses as a biennial um-
    belliferous plant?
I will not venture to deny that it is umbelliferous,
I will only add that it is of a nasty green color, and
    faintly odoriferous.

Now, there is one sin for which a lot of cooks and hostesses are someday going to have to atone,
Which is that they can't bear to cook anything and leave it alone.
No, they see food as something to base a lot of beautiful dreams and romance on,
Which explains lamb chops with pink and blue pants on.
Everything has to be all decorated and garnished
So the guests will be amazed and astarnished,
And whatever you get to eat, it's sprinkled with a lot of good old umbelliferous parsley looking as limp and wistful as Lillian Gish,
And it is limpest, and wistfulest, and also thickest, on fish.
Indeed, I think maybe one reason for the disappearance of Enoch Arden
Was that his wife had an idea that mackerel tasted better if instead of looking like mackerel it looked like a garden.
Well, anyhow, there's the parsley cluttering up your food,
And the problem is to get it off without being rude,
And first of all you try to scrape it off with your fork,
And you might as well try to shave with a cork,
And then you surreptitiously try your fingers,
And you get covered with butter and gravy, but the parsley lingers,
And you turn red and smile at your hostess and compliment her on the recipe and ask her where she found it,
And then you return to the parsley and as a last resort you try to eat around it,

And the hostess says, Oh you are just picking at it, is
    there something wrong with it?
So all you can do is eat it all up, and the parsley along
    with it,
And now is the time for all good parsleyphobes to come
    to the aid of the menu and exhibit their gumption,
And proclaim that any dish that has either a taste or an
    appearance that can be improved by parsley is ipso
    facto a dish unfit for human consumption.

NINE MILES TO THE RAILROAD

The country is a funny place,
I like to look it in the face.
And everywhere I look I see
Some kind of animal or tree.

Indeed, I frequently remark
The country is rather like a park.

The country cows give milk, and moo,
Just like their sisters in the zoo.
The rural squirrel in his rage
Chirks like a squirrel in a cage.

Animals, in their joys and passions,
Like women, follow city fashions.

The horses here pull plows and carts
All day until the sun departs.
In summer, or when fields are frosted,
They work until they are exhausted.

Next, to the track themselves they hie
To be bet upon by the likes of I.

As through the countryside you pass
You look at grass and still more grass.
Grass leers at you where'er you turn
Until your tired eyelids burn.

They ought to break it up, or soften it,
With pretty signs saying, please keep offen it.

I like the country very much.
It's good to hear and smell and touch.
It makes you feel akin with Nature,
Though wobbly on her nomenclature.

I'd free my lungs of city air
If I didn't feel much more important there.

THE STRANGE CASE OF THE DEAD
DIVORCÉE

Once upon a time there was beautiful woman named
    Mrs. Geraldine McGregor Hamilton Garfinkle
    Boyce.

ↄ๏ว

Her first husband, Mr. McGregor, divorced her for in-
    fidelity.

ↄ๏ว

That wasn't his real reason, but he didn't want to blast
    her reputation.

ↄ๏ว

Her second husband, Mr. Hamilton, divorced her for infidelity, too.

∽

He had better grounds, which he was too chivalrous to mention.

∽

Her third husband, Mr. Garfinkle, was a cad.

∽

He prepared a statement for the press setting forth his actual motives for divorcing her.

∽

Her white-haired old mother pled tearfully with him for seven hours, pausing only to telephone her maid to bring over a dozen clean handkerchiefs.

∽

Mr. Garfinkle, if a cad, was a soft-hearted cad.

∽

He destroyed his original damaging statement and informed the press that he was divorcing his wife for infidelity.

∽

It was in June that Mrs. Geraldine McGregor Hamilton Garfinkle become Mrs. Geraldine McGregor Hamilton Garfinkle Boyce.

∽

It was in July that Mr. Boyce slaughtered her with a priceless heirloom, an ice-pick.

∽

At the trial, Mr. Boyce pled guilty.

∽

She was infidelitous, said Mr. Boyce, and I saw red.

∽

Mr. Boyce's lawyer asked him if he didn't have a better excuse.

⁓

Maybe I have, said Mr. Boyce, but my lips are sealed.

⁓

De mortuis, you know, said Mr. Boyce.

⁓

I will only say that she was infidelitous.

⁓

Mr. Boyce was convicted and condemned to die.

⁓

Came Mr. Boyce's Execution Eve.

⁓

The reporters were already strapping their cameras to their ankles when a delegation waited upon the Governor.

⁓

The delegation consisted of Mr. McGregor, Mr. Hamilton and Mr. Garfinkle.

⁓

There are extenuating circumstances in the case of Mr. Boyce, said Mr. McGregor.

⁓

It is time the truth about Geraldine McGregor Hamilton Garfinkle Boyce were told, said Mr. Hamilton.

⁓

I would have told it long ago but for my soft heart, said Mr. Garfinkle.

⁓

Geraldine McGregor Hamilton Garfinkle Boyce was a juleper-in-the-manger, said Mr. McGregor, Mr. Hamilton and Mr. Garfinkle.

⁓

She never drank but half a mint julep, they said.

∽

But when she was offered a mint julep, did she quietly
drink half of it and quietly give the other half to
her husband when he had finished his?

∽

Not Geraldine McGregor Hamilton Garfinkle Boyce!
they said.

∽

She said No thank you, I only want half of one, I'll drink
half of my husband's, they said.

∽

Other women's husbands get a julep and a half, they
said.

∽

Geraldine McGregor Hamilton Garfinkle Boyce's husbands get half a julep, they said.

∽

The Governor pardoned Mr. Boyce forthwith.

∽

Ten minutes later the Governor's butler discovered the
body of the Governor's lady on the veranda.

∽

The ice-pick that protruded from her heart was a priceless heirloom.

THE COMMON COLD

Go hang yourself, you old M.D.!
You shall no longer sneer at me.
Pick up your hat and stethoscope,

Go wash your mouth with laundry soap;
I contemplate a joy exquisite
In never paying you for your visit.
I did not call you to be told
My malady is a common cold.

By pounding brow and swollen lip;
By fever's hot and scaly grip;
By these two red redundant eyes
That weep like woeful April skies;
By racking snuffle, snort, and sniff;
By handkerchief after handkerchief;
This cold you wave away as naught
Is the damnedest cold man ever caught.

Give ear, you scientific fossil!
Here is the genuine Cold Colossal;
The Cold of which researchers dream,
The Perfect Cold, the Cold Supreme.
This honored system humbly holds
The Supercold to end all colds;
The Cold Crusading for Democracy;
The Führer of the Streptococcracy.

Bacilli swarm within my portals
Such as were ne'er conceived by mortals,
But bred by scientists wise and hoary
In some Olympian laboratory;
Bacteria as large as mice,
With feet of fire and heads of ice
Who never interrupt for slumber
Their stamping elephantine rumba.

A common cold, forsooth, gadzooks!
Please to forgive my ribald looks,
But what derision History holds
For the man who belittled the Cold of Colds!

JUST KEEP QUIET AND NOBODY WILL NOTICE

There is one thing that ought to be taught in all the
    colleges,
Which is that people ought to be taught not to go around
    always making apologies.
I don't mean the kind of apologies people make when
    they run over you or borrow five dollars or step on
    your feet,
Because I think that kind is sort of sweet;
No, I object to one kind of apology alone,
Which is when people spend their time and yours apol-
    ogizing for everything they own.
You go to their house for a meal,
And they apologize because the anchovies aren't caviar
    or the partridge is veal;
They apologize privately for the crudeness of the other
    guests,
And they apologize publicly for their wife's housekeep-
    ing or their husband's jests;
If they give you a book by Dickens they apologize be-
    cause it isn't by Scott,
And if they take you to the theater, they apologize for
    the acting and the dialogue and the plot;

They contain more milk of human kindness than the most capacious dairy can,

But if you are from out of town they apologize for everything local and if you are a foreigner they apologize for everything American.

I dread these apologizers even as I am depicting them,

I shudder as I think of the hours that must be spent in contradicting them,

Because you are very rude if you let them emerge from an argument victorious,

And when they say something of theirs is awful, it is your duty to convince them politely that it is magnificent and glorious,

And what particularly bores me with them,

Is that half the time you have to politely contradict them when you rudely agree with them,

So I think there is one rule every host and hostess ought to keep with the comb and nail file and bicarbonate and aromatic spirits on a handy shelf,

Which is don't spoil the denouement by telling the guests everything is terrible, but let them have the thrill of finding it out for themself.

COFFEE WITH THE MEAL

A gentlemanly gentleman, as mild as May,
Entered a restaurant famed and gay.
A waiter sat him in a draughty seat
And laughingly inquired what he'd like to eat.
"Oh I don't want venison, I don't want veal,
But I do insist on coffee with the meal.

Bring me clams in a chilly group,
And a large tureen of vegetable soup,
Steak as tender as a maiden's dream,
With lots of potatoes hashed in cream,
And a lettuce and tomato salad, please,
And crackers and a bit of Roquefort cheese,
But waiter, the gist of my appeal,
Is coffee with, coffee with, coffee with the meal."
The waiter groaned and he wrung his hands;
"Perhaps da headwaiter onderstands."
Said the sleek headwaiter, like a snobbish seal,
"What, monsieur? Coffee with the meal?"
His lip drew up in scornful laughter;
"Monsieur desires a demitasse after!"
The gentleman's eyes grew hard as steel,
He said, "I'm ordering coffee with the meal.
Hot black coffee in a great big cup,
Fuming, steaming, filled right up.
I don't want coffee iced in a glass,
And I don't want a miserable demitasse,
But what I'll have, come woe, come weal,
Is coffee with, coffee with, coffee with the meal."
The headwaiter bowed like a poppy in the breeze;
"Monsieur desires coffee with the salad or the cheese?"
Monsieur said, "Now you're getting warmer;
Coffee with the latter, coffee with the former;
Coffee with the steak, coffee with the soup,
Coffee with the clams in a chilly group;
Yes, and with a cocktail I could do,
So bring me coffee with the cocktail, too.
I'll fight to the death for my bright ideal,
Which is coffee with, coffee with, coffee with the meal."

The headwaiter swiveled on a graceful heel;
"Certainly, certainly, coffee with the meal!"
The waiter gave an obsequious squeal,
"Yes sir, yes sir, coffee with the meal!"
Oh what a glow did Monsieur feel
At the warming vision of coffee with the meal.
One hour later Monsieur, alas!
Got his coffee in a demitasse.

THE RABBITS

Here's a verse about rabbits
That doesn't mention their habits.

THIS IS GOING TO HURT JUST
A LITTLE BIT

One thing I like less than most things is sitting in a
    dentist chair with my mouth wide open,
And that I will never have to do it again is a hope that
    I am against hope hopen.
Because some tortures are physical and some are mental,
But the one that is both is dental.
It is hard to be self-possessed
With your jaw digging into your chest,
So hard to retain your calm
When your fingernails are making serious alterations in
    your life line or love line or some other important
    line in your palm;

So hard to give your usual effect of cheery benignity

When you know your position is one of the two or three
in life most lacking in dignity.

And your mouth is like a section of road that is being
worked on,

And it is all cluttered up with stone crushers and con-
crete mixers and drills and steam rollers and there
isn't a nerve in your head that you aren't being
irked on.

Oh, some people are unfortunate enough to be strung up
by thumbs,

And others have things done to their gums,

And your teeth are supposed to be being polished,

But you have reason to believe they are being demol-
ished,

And the circumstance that adds most to your terror

Is that it's all done with a mirror,

Because the dentist may be a bear, or as the Romans used
to say, only they were referring to a feminine bear
when they said it, an ursa,

But all the same how can you be sure when he takes his
crowbar in one hand and mirror in the other he
won't get mixed up, the way you do when you try
to tie a bow tie with the aid of a mirror, and forget
that left is right and vice versa?

And then at last he says That will be all; but it isn't because he then coats your mouth from cellar to roof

With something that I suspect is generally used to put a
shine on a horse's hoof,

And you totter to your feet and think, Well it's all over
now and after all it was only this once,

And he says come back in three monce.

And this, O Fate, is I think the most vicious circle that
thou ever sentest,
That Man has to go continually to the dentist to keep
his teeth in good condition when the chief reason
he wants his teeth in good condition is so that he
won't have to go to the dentist.

EXPERIENCE TO LET

Experience is a futile teacher,
Experience is a prosy preacher,
Experience is a fruit tree fruitless,
Experience is a shoe-tree bootless.
For sterile wearience and drearience,
Depend, my boy, upon experience.
The burnt child, urged by rankling ire,
Can hardly wait to get back at the fire,
And, mulcted in the gambling den,
Men stand in line to gamble again.
Who says that he can drink or not?
The sober man? Nay nay, the sot.
He who has never tasted jail
Lives well within the legal pale,
While he who's served a heavy sentence,
Renews the racket, not repentance.
The nation bankrupt by a war
Thinks to recoup with just one more;
The wretched golfer, divot-bound,
Persists in dreams of the perfect round;

He who despiseth the airwaves most
The modernest radio doth boast,
Hoping to find, through constant trial
One perfect program on the dial.
Life's little suckers chirp like crickets
While spending their all on losing tickets.
People whose instinct instructs them naught,
But must by experience be taught,
Will never learn by suffering once,
But ever and ever play the dunce.
Experience! Wise men do not need it!
Experience! Idiots do not heed it!
I'd trade my lake of experience
For just one drop of common sense.

OH TO BE ODD!

Hypochondriacs
Spend the winter at the bottom of Florida and the summer on top of the Adirondriacs.
You go to Paris and live on champagne wine and cognac
If you're a dipsomognac.
If you're a manic-depressive
You don't go anywhere where you won't be cheered up, and people say "There, there!" if your bills are excessive.
But you stick around and work day and night and night and day with your nose to the sawmill
If you're nawmill.

I journey not whence nor whither,
I languish alone in a dither;
I journey not to nor fro,
And my dither to me I owe.
I could find a pleasanter name for it
Had I somebody else to blame for it,
But alas that beneath the sun
Dithers are built for one.
This is the song of the dither,
For viol, bassoon or zither,
Till the greenest simpletons wither
This is the song of the dither;
When regular troubles are wrong with you,
Others are guilty along with you;
Dithers are private trouble
Where you privately stew and bubble.
Come hither, somebody, come hither,
Would you care for a share of my dither?
I want somebody else to be mad at;
"Have at you!" to cry, and be had at.
I am tired of being angry at me,
There is room in my dither for three,
There is room in my dither for two;
We could butt at each other and moo;
We could hiss like the serpent, and slither
Through the tropical depths of my dither;
Like bees we could fight along beelines,
Or spit at each other like felines;
I care not who gaineth the laurel,
All I want is a foe and a quarrel.

Alone in my dither I pine.
For the sake of the days of lang syne,
For your white-haired old feyther and mither,
Come along, come along to my dither.
With no foe in my dither but me,
I swoon, I lay doon, and I dee.

REFLECTION ON THE FALLIBILITY
OF NEMESIS

He who is ridden by a conscience
Worries about a lot of nonscience;
He without benefit of scruples
His fun and income soon quadruples.

SONG BEFORE BREAKFAST

Hopeful each morning I arise
And splash the cobwebs from my eyes.
I brush my teeth and scrape my chin
And bravely at the mirror grin.
Sternly I force myself to say,
Huzza! huzza! another day!
Oh happy me! oh lucky I!
Another chance with life to vie!
Another golden opportunity
To rise and shine in this community!
Another target for my aim!
Another whack at wealth and fame!

Almost I feel within me stir
A budding force of character.
Who knows, indeed, but what I might
Perhaps have altered overnight?
Today may be the day, who knows,
That sees me triumph o'er my foes:
Gluttony, simony, and sloth,
And drawing on the tablecloth;
Perjury, arson, envy, pride,
And renting tales of homicide;
Barratry, avarice and wrath,
And blowing bubbles in the bath.
The differences this day may bring!
Perhaps I'll work like anything;
I'll travel to my tasks on foot,
And in the bank the carfare put,
And buy a haircut when I need it,
And if I get a letter, read it,
And every eve improve myself
With Pitkin or the Five Foot Shelf.
The things I want to do, I won't,
And only do the things I don't.
What lordly aspirations dawn
The while I draw my trousers on!
Oh beamish morning, big with hope
And noble tasks with which to cope,
If I should fail you, do not sorrow;
I'll be a better man tomorrow.

POLITICAL REFLECTION

Like an art-lover looking at the Mona Lisa in the Louvre
Is the New York Herald Tribune looking at Mr. Herbert
    Houvre.

FIRST FAMILIES, MOVE OVER!

Carry me back to Ole Virginny,
And there I'll meet a lot of people from New York,
There the Ole Marsa of the Hounds is from Smithtown
    or Peapack or Millbrook,
And the mocking bird makes music in the sunshine ac-
    companied by the rattling shaker and the popping
    cork.

All up and down the old plantation
Socialites are riding hell-for-leather like witches and war-
    locks,
And there is only one thing that keeps the squirearchy
    from being a genuine reproduction,
Which is that the peasantry's hair is kinky so they
    haven't any forelocks so they can't tug their fore-
    locks.

In the evening by the bright light you can hear those
    darkies singing,
How the white folks do enjoy it and call the attention
    of their friends from Piping Rock to the natural
    musical talent of the dusky proletariat.
You can hear those banjos ringing because the hands

have been ordered to exchange their saxophones for banjos,

And they wish they were singing Lookie lookie lookie, here comes Cookie, but their instructions are to sing Swing Low Sweet Chariot.

Oh what is more beautiful and more Southern than a Southern beauty from Philadelphia or Rumson,

And indeed where was Southern beauty before the advent of Schiaparelli and Elizabeth Arden?

And what is more gracious than a hostess calling you you-all in the singular and plural indiscriminately,

And what has more local color than a lovely girl in jodhpurs telling you about her gyarrrden?

Oh the long happy days spent huntin' or shootin' or fishin',

Or in any other sport provided it's lackin' in g's!

Oh the long happy evenings spent sniffing jasmine and poring over the shiny new family Bible,

And figuring out that after all this is really your home because great-grandmother Wilkins was a Filkins and the Filkinses were related by marriage to the Randolphs or the Lees!

So please somebody carry me back to Ole Virginny,

Where gentlemen are gentlemen and a lady is known by the product she endorses,

Where the atmosphere is as Southern as an advertisement for a medium-priced rye whisky,

And where the Virginians from Virginia have to ride automobiles because the Virginians from Long Island are the only ones who can afford to ride horses.

FRAGONARD

There was an old miser named Clarence,
Who simonized both of his parents.
"The initial expense,"
He remarked, "is immense,
But I'll save it on wearance and tearance."

SAVONAROLA OF MAZDA LANE

Mr. Walter Winchell is a highly significant item of con-
temporary Americana
And I think we should try him on our piana.
He is, for instance, the stork
Of New York.
The reportorial activities of Walter
Do not cease at the altar,
But, whether by exercise of his ingenuity or by payment
of a premium,
He seems also to get in on the epithalemium.
The news may be phrased in phrases too recondite
To be intelligible to anybody but a Broadway and Forty-
secondite,
Nevertheless
The whole world knows in October that an heir will in
July your union bless.
In fact, should you be in Mr. Winchell's Who's Who,
Nothing about you is taboo.
Men, do you regularly stay up until daylight
Under the impression that you are thereby crashing the
élite?

Mr. Winchell says nay,
And you will roué the day.
Ladies, do you think you are safe because nobody can
    class you as polyandrous
Without being slandrous?
Your prestige is not sufficiently awesome and solemn
To keep you out of that illegintimate column.
Mr. Winchell is one of God's scourges
To those with extramural urges.
So bravo then for Mr. Winchell, without whose chroni-
    cle of current peccadillos
A lot more of the right people would be this evening on
    the wrong pillows.

ADMIRAL BYRD

Huzza Huzza for Admiral Byrd
About whom many fine things I have heard.
Huzza Huzza for his gallant crew
About whom many fine things I have heard too.
Huzza Huzza for their spirit of Adventia
So very different from Senile Dementia.
And another Huzza for the U.S.A.
Which produces so many heroes like they.

BIRTH COMES TO THE ARCHBISHOP

Ministers
Don't like bar sinisters.
They consider that sort of irregularity

As the height of vulgarity
And go around making remarks
About the need for patrolling the beaches and parks.
They hate to see any deadlock
Between sin and wedlock
And get very nervous
When people omit the marriage service.
They regard as villains
Owners of unauthorized chillains,
A point of view
Which of course doesn't embarrass me or you
But makes things very inconvenient
For many really quite nice girls who may have been just
    a bit lenient.

So although none of us is in danger
Of the arrival of an inexplicable little stranger
Still I think we ought to join with a lot of others
And wish the best of luck to the nation's unmarried
    mothers.

THE STRANGE CASE OF MR. DONNYBROOK'S BOREDOM

Once upon a time there was a man named Mr. Donnybrook.

∽

He was married to a woman named Mrs. Donnybrook.

∽

Mr. and Mrs. Donnybrook dearly loved to be bored.

∽

Sometimes they were bored at the ballet, other times at the cinema.

∾

They were bored riding elephants in India and elevators in the Empire State Building.

∾

They were bored in speakeasies during Prohibition and in cocktail lounges after Repeal.

∾

They were bored by Grand Dukes and garbagemen, debutantes and demimondaines, opera singers and operations.

∾

They scoured the Five Continents and the Seven Seas in their mad pursuit of boredom.

∾

This went on for years and years.

∾

One day Mr. Donnybrook turned to Mrs. Donnybrook.

∾

My dear, he said, we have reached the end of our rope.

∾

We have exhausted every yawn.

∾

The world holds nothing more to jade our titillated palates.

∾

Well, said Mrs. Donnybrook, we might try insomnia.

∾

So they tried insomnia.

∾

About two o'clock the next morning Mr. Donnybrook
said, My, insomnia is certainly quite boring, isn't it?

༄

Mrs. Donnybrook said it certainly was, wasn't it?

༄

Mr. Donnybrook said it certainly was.

༄

Pretty soon he began to count sheep.

༄

Mrs. Donnybrook began to count sheep, too.

༄

After a while Mr. Donnybrook said, Hey, you're counting my sheep!

༄

Stop counting my sheep, said Mr. Donnybrook.

༄

Why, the very idea, said Mrs. Donnybrook.

༄

I guess I know my own sheep, don't I?

༄

How? said Mr. Donnybrook.

༄

They're cattle, said Mrs. Donnybrook.

༄

They're cattle, and longhorns at that.

༄

Furthermore, said Mrs. Donnybrook, us cattle ranchers
is shore tired o' you sheepmen plumb ruinin' our
water.

༄

I give yuh fair warnin', said Mrs. Donnybrook, yuh better
git them woolly Gila monsters o' yourn back across

the Rio Grande afore mornin' or I'm agoin' to
string yuh up on the nearest cottonwood.

∾

Carramba! sneered Mr. Donnybrook. Thees ees free
range, no?

∾

No, said Mrs. Donnybrook, not for sheepmen.

∾

She strung him up on the nearest cottonwood.

∾

Mr. Donnybrook had never been so bored in his life.

AN INTRODUCTION TO DOGS

The dog is man's best friend.
He has a tail on one end.
Up in front he has teeth.
And four legs underneath.

Dogs like to bark.
They like it best after dark.
They not only frighten prowlers away
But also hold the sandman at bay.

A dog that is indoors
To be let out implores.
You let him out and what then?
He wants back in again.

Dogs display reluctance and wrath
If you try to give them a bath.

They bury bones in hideaways
And half the time they trot sideaways.

Dogs in the country have fun.
They run and run and run.
But in the city this species
Is dragged around on leashes.

Dogs are upright as a steeple
And much more loyal than people.
Well people may be reprehensibler
But that's probably because they are sensibler.

INTROSPECTIVE REFLECTION

I would live all my life in nonchalance and insouciance
Were it not for making a living, which is rather a nouci-
     ance.

LINES INDITED WITH ALL THE
DEPRAVITY OF POVERTY

One way to be very happy is to be very rich
For then you can buy orchids by the quire and bacon by
     the flitch.
And yet at the same time
People don't mind if you only tip them a dime.
Because it's very funny
But somehow if you're rich enough you can get away
     with spending water like money

While if you're not rich you can spend in one evening
  your salary for the year
And everybody will just stand around and jeer.
If you are rich you don't have to think twice about buy-
  ing a judge or a horse,
Or a lower instead of an upper, or a new suit, or a divorce,
And you never have to say When,
And you can sleep every morning until nine or ten,
All of which
Explains why I should like very, very much to be very,
  very rich.

I'LL GET ONE TOMORROW

Barber, barber, come and get me;
Hairy torrents irk and fret me.
Hair and hair again appears,
And climbs like ivy round my ears;
Hair across my collar gambols;
Down my neck it wayward ambles;
Ever down it trips and trickles,
Yes, and where it trips, it tickles.
Barber dear, I wish I knew
Why I do not visit you,
Why I grudge the minutes ten
In your sanitary den,
Why I choose to choke on hair
Rather than to mount your chair.
Men no busier than I
Weekly to your office hie;
Men no braver than myself

Confront the armory on your shelf;
Men no wealthier than me
Gladly meet your modest fee,
And for a fraction of a dollar
Keep the jungle off their collar.
I alone am shy and flustered,
A solitary, cowardly custard,
Shaggy as a prize Angora,
Overrun with creeping flora.
Barber, barber, you're in luck;
The bell has rung, the hour has struck.
Sloth is strong, but hair is stronger;
I cannot stand it any longer.
Barber, barber, here I come;
Shake up the odorous bay rum;
Bring on your shears, your scythes, your snippers,
Bring on your crisp, electric clippers;
Employ a dozen extra sweepers;
Bring giant harvesters and reapers;
I warn you that a bumper crop
Waits to overwhelm your shop.
Barber, barber, be verbose,
Be anything, but clip me close;
Leave me razored, leave me scissored,
Leave me hairless as a lizard;
Barber, barber, singe and scald;
Barber, can't you make me bald?
I'd be the happiest of men,
And never think of you again.

PEOPLE

Some people are popular with other people because their
    wit is pointed
And they can sing tenor and are double-jointed
And have had experiences in Papua and the New Heb-
    rides
And have private anecdotes about public celebrides,
And are bright and amusing in the entr'acte
And always do the right thing in backgammon and
    centr'acte.

Other people are unpopular with other people because
    they discuss Bertrand Russell
And keep wanting you to feel their muscle
And point out that your furniture is oak, not mahogany
And tell you all about their ancestors and progeny
And advise you to move to a suburb
And get away from all this tumult and huburb.

Both kinds of people, however, will eventually succumb
    to acidity;
Or perhaps they will be victims of the humidity
Or even approach metempsychosis
Through the various stages of cirrhosis.
But whatever the manner of their passing may be
It's all all right with me.

FAMILY COURT

One would be in less danger
From the wiles of the stranger

If one's own kin and kith
Were more fun to be with.

BERNARR MACFADDEN

Bernarr Macfadden has given the preamble to the Con-
stitution a sequel,
And established the fact that all women are created
physiqual.
What is more, he has logically developed a little-known
theory of Rousseau's;
Viz: that there is a definite connection between fine
torsos and fine trousseaux.
Yes, many a tenor or baritone has succumbed to some
contralto or soprano
Who learned from Mr. Macfadden about mens sana in
corpore sano.
As a publisher he invariably puts his trust
In a picture of a thigh or a bust.
Perhaps the idea was impromptu
But look what he has comptu!
He could now, if he wished, celebrate every Epiphany
By purchasing a fine solitaire diamond from Mr. Tiffany;
Or again, if he so desired, he could buy for each of his
friends on Septuagesima
A steel girder or turret from the works of Bessemer.
That's what the human body if properly exploited is
capable of.
What is this thing called love?

THE MIDDLE OF THE MONTH

Oh, some people grieve for New Year's Eve,
And some for the dog days fiddle;
My moment sublime is the restful time
When the month is at the middle.

Sing tirra lirra loo for the middle of the month,
Which wipes out woes like chamois!
The middle of the month is honey and milk!
The middle of the month is mammy!

Now let us exult,
For the bills of ult.
Are limbo's laughingstocks;
At Fate we scoff,
For a fortnight off
Are the impotent bills of prox.
The first of the month is oyster-gray,
The last of the month is clammy,
But it's tirra lirra loo for the middle of the month,
For the middle of the month is mammy!

Time, fly not back upon thy track!
The past is merely tedium,
And the future, too, so stand still, do,
While the month is at the medium!

Then tirra lirra loo for the middle of the month
And gambol it in like May Day!
The ravenous wolves are toothless now,
The lambs are in their heyday.

Now turn not pale
At the morning mail
Nor shrink when the telephone shrills,
No evil betides
On the blessed Ides,
The lull between the bills!
Oh, the first of the month is oyster-gray
And the last of the month is clammy,
But it's tirra lirra loo for the middle of the month,
For the middle of the month is mammy!

SPRING COMES TO MURRAY HILL

I sit in an office at 244 Madison Avenue,
And say to myself You have a responsible job, havenue?
Why then do you fritter away your time on this doggerel?
If you have a sore throat you can cure it by using a good
    goggeral,
If you have a sore foot you can get it fixed by a chiropo-
    dist,
And you can get your original sin removed by St. John
    the Bopodist,
Why then should this flocculent lassitude be incurable?
Kansas City, Kansas, proves that even Kansas City
    needn't always be Missourible.
Up up my soul! This inaction is abominable.
Perhaps it is the result of disturbances abdominable.
The pilgrims settled Massachusetts in 1620 when they
    landed on a stone hummock.
Maybe if they were here now they would settle my
    stomach.

Oh, if I only had the wings of a bird
Instead of being confined on Madison Avenue I could
soar in a jiffy to Second or Third.

TIME MARCHES ON

You ask me, brothers, why I flinch.
Well, I will tell you, inch by inch.
Is it not proper cause for fright
That what is day will soon be night?
Evenings I flinch the selfsame way,
For what is night will soon be day.
At five o'clock it chills my gore
Simply to know it isn't four.
How Sunday into Monday melts!
And every month is something else.
If Summer on the ladder lingers,
Autumn tramples upon her fingers,
Fleeing before the jostling train
Of Winter, and Spring, and Summer again.
Year swallows year and licks its lips,
Then down the gullet of next year slips.
We chip at Time with clocks and watches;
We flee him in love and double Scotches;
Even as we scatter in alarm
He marches with us, arm in arm;
Though while we sleep, he forward rides,
Yet when we wake, he's at our sides.
While grandly paying no attention to us
He's doing things I hate to mention to us.
Let men walk straight or let them err,

He never leaves them as they were.
While ladies draw their stockings on
The ladies they were are up and gone.
I pen my lines, I finish, I scan them,
I'm not the poet who began them.
Each moment Time, the lord of changers,
Stuffs our skins with ephemeral strangers.
Good heavens, how remote from me
The billion people I used to be!
Flinch with me, brothers, why not flinch,
Shirts caught in the eternal winch?
Come, let us flinch till Time stands still;
Although I do not think he will.
Hark, brothers, to the dismal proof;
The seconds spattering on the roof!

REFLECTION ON BABIES

A bit of talcum
Is always walcum.

A PLEA FOR A LEAGUE OF SLEEP

Some people lead a feverish life,
For they with restlessness are rife.
They revel in labors energetic,
Their fare is healthful and ascetic,
Their minds are keen, their hands are earthy,
Each day they work on something worthy.

Something accomplished, something done,
Comprises their idea of fun.

My life with joy is sometimes fraught,
But mostly when I'm doing naught.
Yea, I could spend my whole career
A pillow underneath my ear.
How wise was he who wittily said
That there is nothing like a bed.
A mattress is what I like to creep on;
The left side is the one I sleep on.

No honester man is to be found
Than he who sleeps the clock around.
Of malice and ambition free,
The more he sleeps, the sleepier he.
No plots and schemes infest his head,
But dreams of getting back to bed.
His spirit bears no worldly taint;
Scratch a sluggard, and find a saint.

Stalin and Hitler while they sleep
Are harmless as a baby sheep;
Tyrants who cause the earth to quake
Are only dangerous when awake.
This world would be a happier place,
And happier the human race,
And all our pilots be less Pontius,
If people spent more time unconscious.

WEDNESDAY MATINEE

Oh, yes, I'd love to go to the play,
But not the Wednesday matinee.
I'd rather work on a crumbling levee
Than cope with a Wednesday theater bevy.
Women, women, and still more women;
A sea of drugstore perfume to swim in;
Tongues like sirens, and tongues like clappers,
And the ripping crackle of candy wrappers:
(A fudge-nut sundae was all their lunch,
They are dying for something sweet to munch;)
And foreheads grow moist and noses glisten,
It's everyone talk, and nobody listen;
Voice beats on voice, and higher and higher
Screams and steams the anarchic choir.
The early-comers sit on the aisle
With their laps in a Himalayan pile,
Every corpulent knee a sentry
Denying to all the right of entry.
The usher glances at laps and knees,
And murmurs, Show me your tickets, please.
The aborigines clatter and clack,
But they're next aisle over and eight rows back.
Thither they march, with candy and wraps,
To be balked by other knees and laps.
The house lights fade, the footlights glow,
The curtain rises. This is the show;
This is the charm, the enchanted flame,
That drew them here from wherever they came.
Over the house no silence falls,
But shopper to shopper desperate calls;

Suburban ladies their tonsils gird,
Determined to have one final word,
Interrupting their own ripe rush
To squelch their neighbors with cries of Hush!
The dialogue dies upon the stage
At the rustle and swish of the program page.
With a wave of applause, terrific, tidal,
They recognize the star, their idol,
Undeterred by the sober fact
That she won't appear till the end of the act.
Now the whisper runs from row to row,
Doesn't the butler look like Joe?
And the mother's the image of Emily, kind of,
And who does the lover put you in mind of?
Now, like the drunkard scenting liquor,
The ladies sniff for dirt, and snicker;
Forgetting now their gum and fudge,
The ladies cackle and leer and nudge,
Rooting in every harmless line
For double-entendre and obscene design;
Yet prompt with handkerchief and tears
The moment a child or a dog appears.
The curtain falls; the play is ended.
Adorable! Dreadful! Stupid! Splendid!
They cry of the play that was unattended,
Unheard, unseen, and uncomprehended.
O matinee mænads, O bulging bacchantes,
I would my pen were as sharp as Dante's,
But as it isn't I simply say
You may keep your Wednesday matinee.

THE PHŒNIX

Deep in the study
Of eugenics
We find that fabled
Fowl, the Phœnix.
The wisest bird
As ever was,
Rejecting other
Mas and Pas,
It lays one egg,
Not ten or twelve,
And when it's hatched,
Out pops itselve.

LINES IN DISPRAISE OF DISPRAISE

I hereby bequeath to the Bide-a-Wee Home all people
    who have statistics to prove that a human
Is nothing but a combination of iron and water and pot-
    ash and albumen.
That may very well be the truth
But it's just like saying that a cocktail is nothing but
    ice and gin and vermouth.
People who go around analyzing
Are indeed very tanalizing.
They always want to get at the bottom
Of everything from spring to ottom.
They can't just look at a Rembrandt or a Bartolozzi
And say, Boy! that's pretty hozzi-tozzi!
No, they have to break it up into its component parts

And reconstruct it with blueprints and charts.
My idea is that while after looking around me and even
  at me I may not be proud of being a human
I object to having attention called to my iron and water
  and potash and albumen.
In the first place, it's undignified,
And in the second place, nothing by it is signified.
Because it isn't potash et cetera that makes people Re-
  publicans or Democrats or Ghibellines or Guelphs,
It's the natural perversity of the people themselfs.
No, no, you old analysts, away with the whole kit and
  kaboodle of you.
I wouldn't even make mincemeat to give to a poodle of
  you.

MORE ABOUT PEOPLE

When people aren't asking questions
They're making suggestions
And when they're not doing one of those
They're either looking over your shoulder or *stepping*
  on your toes
And then as if that weren't enough to annoy you
They employ you.
Anybody at leisure
Incurs everybody's displeasure.
It seems to be very irking
To people at work to see other people not working,
So they tell you that work is wonderful medicine,
Just look at Firestone and Ford and Edison,

And they lecture you till they're out of breath or something
And then if you don't succumb they starve you to death
or something.
All of which results in a nasty quirk:
That if you don't want to work you have to work to earn
enough money so that you won't have to work.

TRAVELER'S REST

I know a renegade hotel,
I also know I hate it well.
An inn so vile, an inn so shameless,
For very disgust I leave it nameless,
Loathing the name I will not utter,
Whose flavor reeks of rancid butter.
Five stories tall this mantrap stands,
With steps outstretched like welcoming hands,
And travelers, weary of their mileage,
Respond to its bright electric smileage.
They park their cars, and praise the Lord
For downy bed and toothsome board.
They pass unwary through its portals,
And every imp in Hades chortles.
Behold the regulars in the lobby;
Expectoration is their hobby.
Behold the loftiest of clerks:
He's manicuring as he works,
And bridles into dapper wrath
At a mild request for a room and bath.

Behold the niftiest of collars
Which murmurs, "That will be six dollars,"
The leer with innuendo rife,
Which says your wife is not your wife.
The doddering, halting elevator,
A contemporary of Poe or Pater.
The impudent boy with step that lags
Who snatches your coins and hides your bags;
The ill-fitting door to the musty room
That smells like a fairly empty tomb;
The bath you crave, being cramped and dusty,
And the Hot that turns out to be cold and rusty,
The towels clammy, the basin black,
And the bed that sags like a postman's back.
The dinner (two dollars and a quarter)
For the porterhouse that tastes like the porter.
The sleepy ascent to the room once more,
And the drunken Lothario next door.
You see that the beds are not turned down,
And you know the bedclothes are dank and brown,
And there isn't a thing to hang your clothes on,
And the sheet you shudder to place your toes on.
You search in vain for a bedside lamp,
You lose your slippers, the rug is damp,
The bulb in the ceiling is all in all,
And the switch is set in the furtherest wall.
A century later the night is past,
And you stagger down to break your fast.
Octoroon coffee, and shiny eggs
Semi-equipped with beaks and legs.
And you reach the desk and surrender your keys,
And the clerk sneers "Thirteen dollars, please,

Seven for meals and six for the room,
Do you know to who you are speaking to whom?
You can fry in hell so long as you pay;
Stop in again when you pass our way!"
I know a renegade hotel.
I also know I hate it well.
I'd name its name with my hand on the Bible,
But for disgust. And the laws of libel.

ARTHUR BRISBANE

Mr. Arthur Brisbane
Considers his country's bane his bane,
He vigorously combats disloyalty
And deprecates royalty,
And though his speech is somewhat informal,
He is a staunch advocate of the normal.
He can pen an editorial
As noble and succinct as the Lincoln Memorial
And in his column, which is widely syndicated,
The man in the street is vindicated.
Because he thought of putting LITTLE words in BIG
    letters,
He is now one of our betters.
He can sit for hour after hour
In a tastily gotten-up flat in the Ritz Tower,
Of which he is owner and proprietor
Because he is such a good wrietor.
I wonder if you and I could assume similar attitudes
If we too knew how to pound the multitude with plati-
    tudes.

RIDING ON A RAILROAD TRAIN

Some people like to hitch and hike;
They are fond of highway travel;
Their nostrils toil through gas and oil,
They choke on dust and gravel.
Unless they stop for the traffic cop
Their road is a fine-or-jail road,
But wise old I go rocketing by;
I'm riding on the railroad.

I love to loll like a limp rag doll
In a peripatetic salon;
To think and think of a long cool drink
And cry to the porter, allons!
Now the clickety-clack of wheel on track
Grows clickety-clackety-clicker:
The line is clear for the engineer
And it mounts to his head like liquor.

Oh give me steel from roof to wheel,
But a soft settee to sit on,
And a cavalcade of commerce and trade
And a drummer to turn the wit on.
Stuyvesant chats with Kelly and Katz,
The professor warms to the broker,
And life is good in the brotherhood
Of an air-conditioned smoker.

With a farewell scream of escaping steam
The boiler bows to the Diesel;
The Iron Horse has run its course
And we ride a chromium weasel;

We draw our power from the harnessed shower,
The lightning without the thunder,
But a train is a train and will so remain
While the rails glide glistening under.

THE STORK

From long descriptions I have heard
I guess this creature is a bird.
I've nothing else of him to say,
Except I wish he'd go away.

THE REBUFFERS

There are some people who if you say something nice to
them,
They certainly don't encourage you to do it twice to
them,
Because you pay them a compliment and they are not
receptive and gracious,
No, they snub you as if you had said something insulting
and outracious.
You say Isn't that a becoming dress!
And they say What, this mess?
And you say something like This evening your eyes are
very beautiful, and the only reason you say it is that
you think this evening their eyes are very beautiful,
And they promptly inform you that they know that you
really think their eyes look like two incompatible

poached eggs, and are just saying the other to be
  dutiful.
Come on Modesty, step up and take the blame;
Thou art responsible, Modesty, for all the innocent little
  compliments strangled in thy name.
And there is one truth which it might be well to remind
  the gruff rebuffer to swallow to the dregs,
Which is that beauty is in the eye of the beholder, and
  the complimenter may indeed have been mistaken,
  because to somebody else maybe the dress was a
  mess, and the eyes were like two incompatible
  poached eggs,
Because everybody who has somebody who thinks they
  are wonderful also has somebody who thinks they
  are terrible,
And all I wish the rebuffers is that they may overhear
  the conversation of their enemies if they find the
  conversation of their friends so unbearable.

REFLECTION ON A WICKED WORLD

Purity
Is obscurity.

MALICE DOMESTIC

A Mrs. Shepherd of Danbury, Conn.,
She tried to steal our cook,
She may have thought to stay anon.,

But now she's in a book!
Oh — Mrs. — Shepherd,
OH! Mrs. SHEPHERD!
I'll hunt you hither, I'll hunt you yon.
Did you really hope to remain anon.?
Didn't you know the chance you took
Making a pass at a poet's cook?

Oh, Mrs. S. of the Nutmeg State,
No human shame she knew,
Her carnal appetites to sate,
Our home she walked into.
Oh — Mrs. — Shepherd!
OH! Mrs. SHEPHERD!
By hook and by crook and by telephone
You attempted to rape us of our own.
You ruptured the laws of God and man
And made a pass at Matilda Ann.

Then here's a health to Matilda Ann
Whose soups are soundly peppered,
Whose commonest meats are godlike feats,
Who resisted Mrs. Shepherd.
But — Oh — Mrs. — Shepherd!
OH! Mrs. SHEPHERD!
You ruptured the laws of man and God
When in our kitchen you softly trod.
You tiptoed hither, you tiptoed yon,
You fondly hoped to remain anon.,
But householders all, the nation over,
Shall hear the name of the lawless rover
Who by telephone and by hook and crook

Attempted to alienate our cook.
Go back to your home in Danbury, Conn.,
And carry this curse to ponder on:
I hope that your soup is washy-wishy,
Your salad sandy, your butter fishy,
Your sirloins fried and your whitebait boiled,
Your omelets burned and your sherbets oiled,
Till all your neighbors in Danbury, Conn.,
As they watch the Shepherds grow feeble and wan,
Say "She should have thought of the chance she took,
Making a pass at a poet's cook."

HYMN TO THE SUN AND MYSELF

Well! Well!
The day's at the morn!
Dandy old day!
Dandy old morn!
Oh! Look!
The hillside's dew-pearled!
Nicely old hillside!
Nicely dew-pearled!
And oh! Look!
The snail's on the thorn!
Lucky old snail!
Lucky old thorn!
Well! Well!
All's right with the world!
Hurrah for the right!
Hurrah for the world!

For oh! what a day it is today, my lads!
Oh! my lads, what a day it is today!
At 11:07 A.M. I'll be 27¾ years old,
An age dear to me because it was once passed through
      by Edna St. Vincent Millay.
Oh what fun to be young and healthy and alive
And privileged to do some of the work of the world from
      nine to five!
Oh let me be truly thankful for every one of those 27¾
      years;
For not having been run over by the Lexington Avenue
      Express or gored by runaway steers;
For not having been able to afford a passage on the
      Titanic,
And for not having had any money to lose in the recent
      stock market panic;
For never having written a best-seller, only to be wounded
      by the critics;
For never having gotten impeached for making millions
      in dirty politics;
For never having made any enemies by getting ahead too
      speedily;
For not finding the world at my feet while still as young
      as Lindbergh or Gertrude Ederle;
Above all let me be thankful for something rarer than
      gold —
Viz: that at 11:07 A.M. I'll be 27¾ years old.
Oh let my future be as lucky as my past!
Oh let every day for a long time not be my last!

THE BANQUET

Oh, here we are at the mammoth banquet
To honor the birth of the great Bosanquet!
Oh give a look at the snowy napery,
The costly flowers, the sumptuous drapery,
Row on row of silver utensils
Poised for action like salesmen's pencils,
Waiters gaudy as sugar plums,
Every waiter with seven thumbs,
Stream upon stream of gaudy bunting,
And lady commuters lion hunting,
The gleaming teeth at the speaker's table,
The clattering, chattering, battering babel.
Sit we here in the great unquiet
And brood awhile on the evening's diet.
As soggy and dull as good advice,
The butter floats in the melting ice.
In a neighboring morgue, beyond salvation,
The celery waits identification.
Huddled thick in an open vault,
Mummified peanuts moult their salt.
Out of the napkin peers a roll,
With the look of a lost and hardened soul.
The cocktail sauce, too weak to roister,
Fails to enliven the tepid oyster.
The consommé, wan as Elizabeth Barrett,
Washes over a drowning carrot.
Next, with its sauce of Mdvi-Tartar,
The sole, or flounder, or is it a garter?
Ho! fresh from the ranchos of Avignon,
O'Sullivan's Rubber filet mignon;

Parsley potatoes, as tempting as soap,
String beans, hemp beans, and beans of rope.
And the waiter would sooner serve you his daughter
Than give you another glass of water.
Pineapple salad next, by George!
That ought to raise your sunken gorge!
And green ice cream, sweet frozen suet,
With nuts and raisins sprinkled through it.
At sight of vari-colored gâteaux
The innards reel, as on a bateau.
At last the little cups belated
Of coffee dated, or inundated.
Chairs creak as half a thousand rumps
Twist them around with backward bumps,
A thousand eyes seek out, as one,
The beaming chairman on his throne.
He rises luminous through the smoke
Of banquet tobacco, or poison oak.
He bows, he coughs, he smiles a bit,
He sparkles with imitable wit —
Rabbi Ben Ezra, fly with me;
The almost worse is yet to be.
Let us arise and leave this banquet —
And by the way, Rabbi, who was Bosanquet?

PEDIATRIC REFLECTION

Many an infant that screams like a calliope
Could be soothed by a little attention to its diope.

Vanity, vanity, all is vanity
That's any fun at all for humanity.
Food is vanity, so is drink,
And undergarments of gossamer pink,
P. G. Wodehouse, and long vacations,
Going abroad, and rich relations,
The kind of engagements you want to keep,
A hundred honors, and twelve hours' sleep.
Vanities all — Oh Worra, worra!
Rooted in Sodom and Gomorrah.

Vanity, vanity, all is vanity
That's any fun at all for humanity.
That is the gist of the prophet's case,
From Bishop Cannon to Canon Chase.
The prophets chant and the prophets chatter,
But somehow it never seems to matter,
For the world hangs on to its ancient sanity
And orders another round of vanity.
Then Hey! for Gomorrah! and Nonny! for Sodom!
Marie! the Chanel model for Modom!

A BRIEF GUIDE TO NEW YORK

In New York beautiful girls can become more beautiful
    by going to Elizabeth Arden
And getting stuff put on their faces and waiting for it
    to harden,

And poor girls with nothing to their names but a letter or
    two can get rich and joyous
From a brief trip to their loyous.
So I can say with impunity
That New York is a city of opportunity.
It also has many fine theaters and hotels,
And a lot of taxis, buses, subways and els,
Best of all, if you don't show up at the office or at a tea
    nobody will bother their head
They will just think you are dead.
That's why I really think New York is exquisite.
And someday I'm going to pay it a visit.

GERVAISE

There was a young belle of old Natchez
Whose garments were always in patchez.
When comment arose
On the state of her clothes,
She drawled, When Ah itchez, Ah scratchez!

INCOMPETENT AND IMMATERIAL

There was a lady loved a gent,
But her reward was meager.
Said her gentleman friend to his gentleman friends,
The lady's overeager.

There was a lady loved a gent,
She held her backbone rigid.
Said her gentleman friend to his gentleman friends,
The lady's far too frigid.

There was a lady loved herself,
But equipped with Cold and Hot.
Said her gentleman friends to their gentleman friends,
Whatever it is, she's got.

Oh let us laugh at the lines above,
Less precious than pearls and rubies —
Telling the ladies what ladies know,
That gentlemen all are boobies.

SEDATIVE REFLECTION

Let the anxious wooer cure insomnia
By murmuring AMOR VINCIT OMNIA.

LINES IN PRAISE OF A DATE MADE
PRAISEWORTHY SOLELY BY
SOMETHING VERY NICE
THAT HAPPENED
TO IT

As through the calendar I delve
I pause to rejoice in April twelve.

Yea, be I in sickness or be I in health
My favorite date is April twealth.

It comes upon us, as a rule,
Eleven days after April Fool,

And eighteen days ahead of May Day
When spring is generally in its heyday.

Down in New Mexico the chaparral
Is doing nicely by the twelfth of Aparral,

And Bay State towns such as Lowell and Pepperell
Begin to bloom on the twelfth of Epperell.

But regardless of the matter of weather,
There isn't any question whether.

No, not till the trumpet is blown by Gabriel
Shall we have such a day as the twelfth of Abriel.

SUCH AN OLD THEME, BUT SUCH
FRESH DISTRESS

There is a woman —
There is a vulture
Who circles above
The carcass of culture —
I beg your pardon,
Mrs. Dora Schultz Malone Le Baron Van Arden,
I've a rush of work, such a devastating plight,
I'm afraid that dinner's out of the question tonight.
Roumanians and Serbs
Get on my nerbs;

Pagliacci Russians,
Romanoff repercussions,
Croats and Slovenes
And London epicenes —
Oh Lummy!
They do things to my tummy.
Dear Mrs. Van Arden,
I do beg your pardon,
But you have had Mr. Malone (number one), Mr. Le
     Baron (number two), and Mr. Van A. (number
     three),
And now your Balkans and things; surely you don't need
     me.
Mrs. Van Arden is fond of books —
Sometimes at them she even looks.
There's a frightfully clever young poet coming next
     week —
Oh, quite, quite unique.
Very good-looking, but not above his station;
He's invented a different kind of punctuation.
And the following week a rather thrilling Pole,
Brutal, my dear, but a solid mass of soul.
You'll never forget
The marvelous way he plays the flageolet —
There's a spirituality about the Slav
That none of us Anglo-Saxons seems to have.
In Mrs. Van Arden's hair Titian is now the determinant;
Mrs. Van Arden's smile and her youth are equally per-
     manent.
She is young, she is young, she is young. Only a cad
     would note
The hands and the throat.

It's no fault of hers that my flesh begins to creep
At the sight of a spring sheep.
Oh Mrs. Van Arden,
I beg, I beg your pardon,
I must wrench myself away from your charming salon;
My genius — you know my genius — whispers "Allons."

SO PENSEROSO

Come, megrims, mollygrubs and collywobbles!
Come, gloom that limps, and misery that hobbles!
Come also, most exquisite melancholiage,
As dark and decadent as November foliage!
I crave to shudder in your moist embrace,
To feel your oystery fingers on my face.
This is my hour of sadness and of soulfulness,
And cursed be he who dissipates my dolefulness.
The world is wide, isn't it?
The world is roomy.
Isn't there room, isn't it,
For a man to be gloomy?
Bring me a bathysphere, kindly,
Maybe like Beebe's,
Leave me alone in it, kindly,
With my old heebie-jeebies.
I do not desire to be cheered,
I desire to retire, I am thinking of growing a beard,
A sorrowful beard, with a mournful, a dolorous hue in it,
With ashes and glue in it.
I want to be drunk with despair,
I want to caress my care,

I do not wish to be blithe,
I wish to recoil and writhe,
I will revel in cosmic woe,
And I want my woe to show.
This is the morbid moment,
This is the ebony hour.
Aroint thee, sweetness and light!
I want to be dark and sour!
Away with the bird that twitters!
All that glitters is jitters!
Roses, roses are gray,
Violets cry Boo! and frighten me.
Sugar is diabetic,
And people conspire to brighten me.
Go hence, people, go hence!
Go sit on a picket fence!
Go gargle with mineral oil,
Go out and develop a boil!
Melancholy is what I brag and boast of,
Melancholy I mean to make the most of,
You beaming optimists shall not destroy it.
But while I am it, I intend to enjoy it.
Go, people, feed on kewpies and soap,
And remember, please, that when I mope, I mope!

INTEROFFICE MEMORANDUM

The only people who should really sin
Are the people who can sin with a grin,
Because if sinning upsets you,
Why, nothing at all is what it gets you.

Everybody certainly ought to eschew all offences however
venial

As long as they are conscience's menial.

Some people suffer weeks of remorse after having com-
mitted the slightest peccadillo,

And other people feel perfectly all right after feeding
their husbands arsenic or smothering their grand-
mother with a pillow.

Some people are perfectly self-possessed about spending
their lives on the verge of delirium tremens,

And other people feel like hanging themselves on a coat-
hook just because they took that extra cocktail and
amused their fellow guests with recitations from the
poems of Mrs. Hemans.

Some people calmly live a barnyard life because they find
monogamy dull and arid,

And other people have sinking spells if they dance twice
in an evening with a lady to whom they aren't
married.

Some people feel forever lost if they are riding on a bus
and the conductor doesn't collect their fare,

And other people ruin a lot of widows and orphans and
all they think is, Why there's something in this
business of ruining widows and orphans, and they
go out and ruin some more and get to be a millionaire.

Now it is not the purpose of this memorandum, or song,

To attempt to define the difference between right and
wrong;

All I am trying to say is that if you are one of the
unfortunates who recognize that such a difference
exists,

Well, you had better oppose even the teensiest temptation with clenched fists,
Because if you desire peace of mind it is all right to do wrong if it never occurs to you that it is wrong to do it,
Because you can sleep perfectly well and look the world in the eye after doing anything at all so long as you don't rue it,
While on the other hand nothing at all is any fun
So long as you yourself know it is something you shouldn't have done.
There is only one way to achieve happiness on this terrestrial ball,
And that is to have either a clear conscience, or none at all.

COMPLAINT TO FOUR ANGELS

Every night at sleepy-time
Into bed I gladly climb.
Every night anew I hope
That with the covers I can cope.

Adjust the blanket fore and aft,
Swallow next a soothing draught;
Then a page of Scott or Cooper
May induce a healthful stupor.

Oh, the soft luxurious darkness,
Fit for Morgan, or for Harkness!

Traffic dies along the street.
The light is out. So are your feet.

Adjust the blanket aft and fore,
Sigh, and settle down once more.
Behold, a breeze! The curtains puff.
One blanket isn't quite enough.

Yawn and rise and seek your slippers,
Which, by now, are cold as kippers.
Yawn, and stretch, and prod yourself,
And fetch a blanket from the shelf.

And so to bed again, again,
Cozy under blankets twain.
Welcome warmth and sweet nirvana
Till eight o'clock or so mañana.

You sleep as deep as Keats or Bacon;
Then you dream and toss and waken.
Where is the breeze? There isn't any.
Two blankets, boy, are one too many.

O stilly night, why are you not
Consistent in your cold and hot?
O slumber's chains, unlocked so oft
With blankets being donned or doffed!

The angels who should guard my bed
I fear are slumbering instead.
O angels, please resume your hovering;
I'll sleep, and you adjust the covering.

OLD MEN

People expect old men to die,
They do not really mourn old men.
Old men are different. People look
At them with eyes that wonder when . . .
People watch with unshocked eyes . . .
But the old men know when an old man dies.

THE INDIVIDUALIST

Once there was a man named Jarvis Gravel who was just
    a man named Jarvis Gravel except for one thing:
He hated spring.
And this was because once a Communist had said Come
    on down to Union Square, it's May Day,
And Jarvis went, thinking he had said Come on down
    to Union Square, it's pay day.
So from then on anything at all vernal
Was to him strictly infernal.
When he saw the first crocus poke its head up
He'd get a shovel and dig the entire bed up,
And he bought a horse and galloped back and forth
Tipping off the worms when the first robin started North.
To love the way of a man with a maid in the moonlight
    was something he never learnt,
And he spent a lot of beautiful balmy evenings moving
    FRESH PAINT signs from park benches that were
    freshly painted to ones that weren't,
And when he finally did marry a girl who made his pulses
    quicken

It was merely because her name was Gale Winterbottom
  and she was no spring chicken,
And one day during the worm-warning season he came
  home hungry after a hard day in the stirrup,
And she served him waffles and he objected to the May-
  pole syrup,
So she shot him through the heart, but his last words
  were ecstatic.
He said Thank you honey, it was thoughtful of you to
  use the autumnatic.

A CAROL FOR CHILDREN

God rest you, merry Innocents,
Let nothing you dismay,
Let nothing wound an eager heart
Upon this Christmas day.

Yours be the genial holly wreaths,
The stockings and the tree;
An aged world to you bequeaths
Its own forgotten glee.

Soon, soon enough come crueler gifts,
The anger and the tears;
Between you now there sparsely drifts
A handful yet of years.

Oh, dimly, dimly glows the star
Through the electric throng;
The bidding in temple and bazaar
Drowns out the silver song.

The ancient altars smoke afresh,
The ancient idols stir;
Faint in the reek of burning flesh
Sink frankincense and myrrh.

Gaspar, Balthazar, Melchior!
Where are your offerings now?
What greetings to the Prince of War,
His darkly branded brow?

Two ultimate laws alone we know,
The ledger and the sword —
So far away, so long ago,
We lost the infant Lord.

Only the children clasp his hand;
His voice speaks low to them,
And still for them the shining band
Wings over Bethlehem.

God rest you, merry Innocents,
While innocence endures.
A sweeter Christmas than we to ours
May you bequeath to yours.